Tapestry
AND
BEADWORK

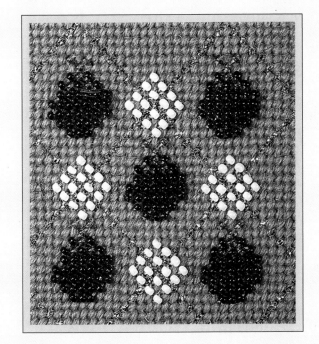

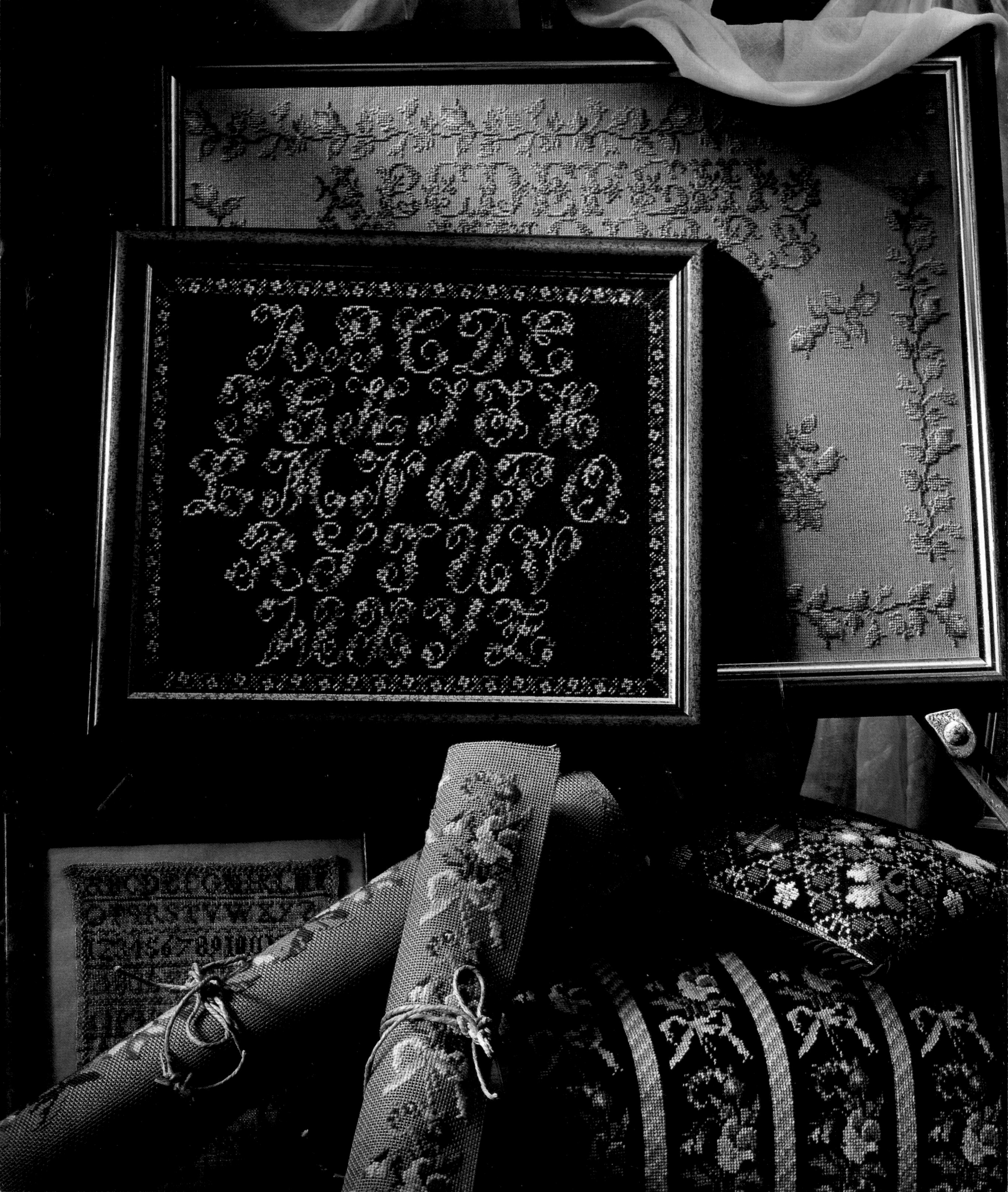

Tapestry

AND

BEADWORK

CANVASWORK PROJECTS FOR THE HOME

Julia Hickman

photography by Tim Hill • styling by Zöe Hill

David & Charles

DEDICATION

To Peter, Hayes and Nell

A DAVID & CHARLES BOOK

© Text, designs and charts Julia Hickman 1993
© Photography David & Charles 1993

First published 1993

A catalogue record for this book is available from the
British Library.

ISBN 0 7153 9960 8

Charts by Angela Kirk and Ethan Danielson
Diagrams by Susan Rentoul

Typeset by Central Southern Typesetters Eastbourne
and printed in Italy by
Nuovo Istituto Italiano d'Arti Grafiche–Bergamo
for David & Charles
Brunel House Newton Abbot Devon

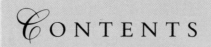

CONTENTS

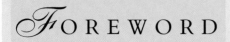

FOREWORD

I was brought up in a delightfully vague and artistic world – my mother had been a child prodigy, who sang and played the piano and flute professionally, and my father was a keen collector of decorative objects. So our home was alive with music, and my sister and I were lucky enough to be surrounded by beautiful paintings, furniture and objets d'art, which helped to stimulate early artistic skills in both of us. In my case this later developed into an interest in embroidery on canvas, correctly known as canvas work but more often referred to as tapestry (in imitation of traditional woven textiles).

As children, we were able to indulge our artistic obsessions at a wonderfully eccentric theatrical school – much to the detriment of our scholastic work as it turned out. The school was based in a most beautiful house which incorporated almost every sort of interior design style, with wonderfully elegant rooms, including a grand marble ballroom – it proved to be an education to both the mind and the eye, and a formative influence.

After leaving school I joined a well-known fashion house and worked for them for many years, learning about design, colour and promotion. When I left, to bring up my family, I still took a keen interest in any hand-made craft. While my family were young I became increasingly interested in canvas embroidery and worked a few Florentine patterns, but found them too repetitive. I wondered if there was

Our house and garden at Little Lodge which opens under the National Gardens Scheme once a year.
(Photograph © Jarrold Colour Publications/J.A. Brooks for the Gardeners' Royal Benevolent Society)

something more interesting, perhaps something using different stitches, and then I discovered that there is more to canvas work than just straight stitch and tent stitch and that beadwork gives tapestry yet another dimension. As my interest grew, my daughter, then under five, and I would go to a local needlework class once a week, which eventually led me to a City and Guilds Embroidery course where I discovered a whole range of fascinating textured stitches. I started to teach small groups, and many of the people attending asked for designs to work on between courses, so I began to work out patterns for them to take away. This led to the birth of my embroidery company, Stitchery.

From this small beginning, Stitchery has become an international company. Our designs are sold in stores and specialist shops throughout the United Kingdom, as well as in Europe, the Far East, Australia, New Zealand and the United States. It has been an exciting time for all of us involved and we have been able to watch the growth of a refreshing new awareness of all forms of decorative crafts, particularly for the home.

Almost anyone who is interested in gardening is also likely to be keen on redesigning the interior of their home, have an interest in cooking and will probably also have a hobby in one of the crafts, such as needlework. The link seems to be in the use of colour and texture: while the gardener plans plant associations, an embroiderer can do the same with yarns, a cook can experiment with different foods and there seems to be no limit to new ideas for decorating the interior of our homes.

There does not seem to be a moment when I am not looking for inspiration either for Stitchery designs or for my garden. Just a few moments spent looking at plants and their colours can be all that is needed to help start a new project or rearrange a section of a flower border. There are other sources of inspiration, however, such as antique embroidered textiles, eastern ceramics and the colours of oriental fabrics. Given a little wool and canvas, I am

The author in her garden

happy to experiment with patterns and colour for hours, trying to turn some of these compositions into a tapestry design.

Embroidery as a pastime is enjoyed nowadays by both men and women, indeed the first design my company ever sold was to a man. We have many men on our mailing list and even my husband finds it therapeutic and relaxing to occasionally work a piece of tapestry for us (when pushed!). We have an active and lively response from our male stitchers, who always seem to produce neat and accurate work. They do not feel embarrassed or self-conscious that this may seem a traditionally feminine activity. Indeed, they recognise that there is nothing more satisfying than having a piece of tapestry at hand to pick up and sew quietly when they are under pressure. Similarly, I hope that there may be a design in this book that will give you hours of enjoyable and relaxing stitching and then, when completed, will be a pleasure to look at for years to come.

$\mathcal{H}$OW TO $\mathcal{B}$EGIN

$\mathcal{C}$anvas embroidery should be a pleasure to work, and a few basic rules and tips will help you to achieve hours of enjoyment. The most important considerations are the yarn colours, the type of canvas – and a relaxed attitude to your work. The techniques of embroidery are important but they certainly should not override the actual enjoyment. The next few pages provide a guide to what is available and how to produce a successful end result. Canvas embroidery will certainly make you feel relaxed, so enjoy it.

Canvas

Any piece of finished canvas embroidery will have taken hours to complete, so it is worth investing in the best quality canvas to ensure it will last. In this book two types of canvas are used: single (mono) and double.

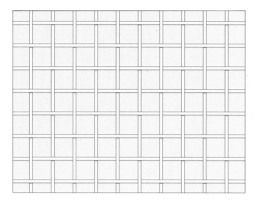

Single canvas showing the single threads running in both directions

Single canvas is woven with a single thread running in both directions and is graded according to the number of threads to each inch (or 10cm). It comes in two colours, either undyed antique-brown or dyed white, and in two qualities, polished or unpolished. The undyed antique-brown polished canvas is the best to work on; it is easy to pull yarn through the polished threads and the antique-brown makes a softer background colour to work with than the white. Unpolished canvas can tear the yarns with its rough threads and be uncomfortable to hold and to sew. White polished canvas is a better choice for people who have poor eyesight as the weave is easier to see; it can also be the best choice with very pale yarns.

Double canvas has a pair of threads running in both directions. It is used for the beadwork in this book, as the double threads hold the beads in place well and the background is easy to fill in with tent stitch.

Double canvas showing a pair of threads running in both directions

Before buying any canvas, work out the design area and make sure there is at least a 2in (5cm) seam allowance all round the design for stretching and making up.

Yarns

All the designs in this book use Appleton yarns, which come in either small skeins or larger hanks. Cut hanks twice into two halves, making lengths of roughly 33in (84cm) and cut similar lengths from a skein. Appleton yarn comes in two thicknesses: crewel wool and tapestry wool. Crewel wool is a fine two-ply yarn that can be used as a single strand for the very finest embroidery or as up to six strands used together on coarser canvas. Crewel wool is very versatile and hard-wearing; it can lie very flat when worked and covers the canvas well. It is ideal for textured stitches on canvas because it allows you to choose the number of strands of yarn required to cover the threads of canvas. For example, small delicate stitches might only need a strand or two to cover the canvas whilst longer stitches might require five or six strands. If several strands are used, colours can be mixed in the needle to create blends and contrasts.

Crewel wool can sometimes be a little fluffy. If it is, draw the strands firmly

between your finger and thumb several times before threading the needle. Keep the strands as untwisted as possible when sewing, so that the threads lie parallel to each other on the canvas. This is especially important for straight stitches. If the yarn starts to twist, turn the needle between finger and thumb until the strands are parallel again. Never re-use yarn which has been unpicked as it will be thin and will spoil the look of the finished work. Similarly, if you notice the yarn becoming over-used and thin, discard it and begin with new yarn.

Tapestry wool is a four-ply yarn, possibly easier for the less experienced worker as only one strand is used on the 12 holes to the inch (46 holes/10cm) size canvas which is used for many of the designs in this book. Two strands or more can be used for making rugs.

Appleton yarns have been used exclusively in this book because they offer such a subtle and extensive range of colours and the yarns are delightful to work with. When buying Appleton yarns, make sure you always match the numbers and not just the names of the colours, as there are for example, nine, different shades under the name Flame Red, each one with a different number.

If you are unable to find Appleton yarns, there is a conversion chart for Coats New Anchor yarns on page 125.

Needles

A tapestry needle is used for canvas work. It has a blunt end and a large eye, and is available from size 16, the largest, to size 26, the smallest. The yarn must pass through the eye with ease and the needle should not be too large as it will distort the threads of the canvas as it passes through. For the canvas sizes used in this book you will need either a size 18 or size 20 needle.

A straw needle is a long fine pointed needle used for general household repairs. A size 9 is very fine and is small enough to thread beads onto.

Getting started

Before you begin to work your design, it is essential to find the centre of the canvas and divide it into quarters. This makes it easy to work from a chart as both the canvas and chart can then be worked in sections. To find the centre, fold the canvas in half in both directions and mark the grooves with an HB pencil or by working a tacking thread between the two central threads of the canvas in each direction.

The canvas can be either bound with masking tape around the edges or turned and stitched to stop it fraying. All tapestry tends to pull as it is worked and, as a result, can get out of shape. This problem can be partly solved by the use of a frame, which may also help to speed up the work as two hands can be used to stitch. An out-of-shape canvas can be rectified by stretching (page 118).

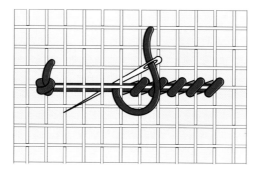

To start stitching leave the knot on the front of the canvas and stitch towards it

To start, make a knot at the end of the yarn and pull the yarn through the canvas with the knot on the right side about 1in (3cm) from where you start stitching. Stitch toward the knot to secure the wool on the back of the canvas; cut the knot when you reach it.

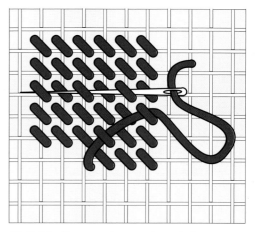

To finish off, weave the yarn through the worked stitches on the back of the canvas

To finish off a strand of yarn, weave it into the back of the worked stitches for about 1in (3cm), first in one and then in another direction. Trim the strand close to the stitches and do not leave loose ends as these may get worked through to the front as stitching continues.

Changing the design size

Any design can be enlarged very easily by working it onto a canvas with a larger mesh than that suggested. Similarly, working on a smaller-size canvas will reduce the size of the design. In both cases, it will be necessary to work a small section of the canvas as a sample to assess the coverage of the yarn and the number of strands to use.

Reading a chart

Stitching a design from a chart can be so satisfying that many needleworkers work only from charts. A good chart enables the embroiderer to complete a project accurately, stitch for stitch, and opens up the possibility of working many different and interesting textured stitches.

In this book, you will find two different types of chart. Where only one stitch is used, one square of the chart represents one stitch to be worked onto the canvas. Where more than one stitch is used, each line on the grid represents one thread of the canvas, so the stitches are shown on the chart just as they will be worked on the canvas.

Both types of chart are easy to follow even if you have never worked from charts before. Once the basic principle is understood, you are unlikely to want to return to printed tapestry canvases.

Adapting charts

Charts are very adaptable and can be enlarged by repeating more of the design, or reduced by omitting part of the pattern. A small section of the pattern can be adapted to make a small item such as a pincushion or glasses case. It is worth experimenting by combining or changing the charts and patterns. Also, it is fun to work out new colour combinations.

Using a roller frame

To produce a finished canvas which has a good even tension and neat stitches, it is advisable to use a roller frame. Although this is not an essential piece of equipment, it does help to keep the canvas evenly stretched and is especially useful when working designs with a variety of stitches which are more likely to distort the canvas. A roller frame also makes it possible to use the correct method of stitching, with one hand feeding the needle up through the canvas and the other returning it down to form the stitch.

Canvases which have been stitched without a frame, or where the stitches are worked in one movement from the front with one hand, are more likely to be badly distorted and difficult to stretch. Never use a round embroidery hoop, which would distort the canvas where

the two rings lock together and damage worked stitches.

The frame should be wide enough to take the width of your canvas, but any reasonable length can be accommodated by rolling the spare canvas round the rollers. Worked and unworked areas of canvas may be rolled up.

Find and mark the centre of the canvas at the top and bottom, and then mark the centre point of the webbing on each of the two rollers. Match the centre points and stitch the canvas to the webbing on the top and bottom roller, working outwards from the centre to each side so the canvas is held firmly to the webbing. Then roll up the canvas so that the area to be worked is held tightly between the rollers, and tighten the screws on the side pieces. The canvas is then ready to be worked.

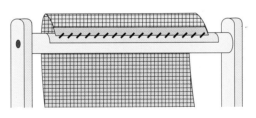

Stitch canvas to webbing, matching the centre of the canvas to the centre of the webbing

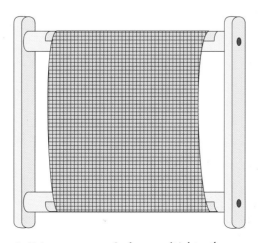

Roll the canvas onto the frame and tighten the screws ready for work

How to make a template

For an awkward shape or a piece of upholstered furniture, you will need to make a template, which will give you a guide to the quantities of yarn and size of canvas that will be required. If the furniture to be covered needs re-upholstering, have this done before the template is made, or allow for the size of the extra stuffing. Often a professional upholsterer will make a template for you and will mount your finished work onto the furniture.

To make a template, use a piece of muslin, old sheeting or lining fabric which is larger than the article to be upholstered. Find the centre lines of the cloth by folding the fabric in both directions and marking the horizontal and vertical lines with a pencil. Measure and find the centre of the item of furniture to be upholstered and lay the piece of marked fabric onto it, matching the two centres. Smooth over and temporarily secure the fabric to the furniture with large running stitches or pins. Carefully mark on the fabric with a pencil around the outside edge of the area to be worked, adding an allowance for an unworked area to be tucked in underneath – there should be at least 2in (5cm) allowance all round.

Find the centre of the canvas by folding in half in both directions and marking the horizontal and vertical lines with a tacking thread, then match the centre lines of the template to the centre of the canvas. Mark the template pattern onto the canvas using a brightly coloured thread and tacking stitches. Keep the template in case the pattern needs adjusting when finished. Do not cut the canvas until after the stitching has been completed and the piece has been stretched back into shape.

Chapter One

REPEATING PATTERNS

*A*NYBODY *who has done the smallest amount of tapestry will have accumulated some leftover yarns, and anyone who is very keen will have amassed many colours. The more designs you work, the more yarn you collect, and the simple repeating patterns in this chapter are an excellent way of using up these spare yarns.*

Amongst my collection of fragments of half-worked sample patterns,

there are several which I have copied from cushions, footstools or chairs in friends' houses. Whenever I have asked where these patterns came from, the answer has been that they have been passed down through the family by mothers, mothers-in-law and aunts. Some also have interesting stories associated with them. For instance, the Queen Mary's Tree pattern (opposite) was allegedly worked by Mary Queen of Scots.

Several of the patterns in this chapter have been conceived solely for using up odd scraps of different coloured yarns. All the patterns use simple stitches; the excitement and interest lies in choosing and mixing the colours for each small part of the pattern. I hope these patterns will inspire you to find a piece of furniture which might need re-upholstering or to use the pattern for something smaller like a glasses case, pincushion or even a small needlecase.

All the patterns were worked on a mono de luxe canvas, 12 holes to the inch (46 holes/10cm), in antique colour for darker yarns or white for the paler yarns. Tapestry wool was used to work the stitches.

This design was allegedly first worked by Mary Queen of Scots on the corner of a handkerchief, using a strand of her red hair for thread, whilst in prison at Fotheringhay Castle. An example of this pattern also turned up amongst some sample pieces from a Mrs Evershed, who ran a shop in London's South Molton Street between 1895 and the 1950s. Many of Mrs Evershed's samples and patterns are now in the archives of the WHI Tapestry Shop in Pimlico Road, London where they are used as inspiration for modern designs.

This design is worked in tent stitch with the border in straight gobelin. (For stitch instructions see pages 123–124.) Each line on the chart represents one thread of canvas.

SIZE 13 × 11in (33 × 28cm)

MATERIALS 17 × 15in (43 × 38cm) mono de luxe antique canvas, 12 holes to the inch (46 holes/10cm), or a piece of canvas 4in (10cm) larger than the area to be worked
Size 18 tapestry needle
Appleton tapestry wool (use one strand) – suggested colour combinations:

①	BRIGHT CHINA BLUE	741
	BRIGHT CHINA BLUE	743
②	DULL ROSE PINK	145
	ROSE PINK	754
③	MAUVE	603
	ROSE PINK	5751
④	HERALDIC GOLD	843
	BRIGHT YELLOW	511
⑤	FLAME RED	206
	CORAL	863
⑥	HONEYSUCKLE	696
	HONEYSUCKLE	694
⑦	FLAME RED	205
	FLAMINGO	621
⑧	MID BLUE	155
	MID BLUE	153
⑨	AUTUMN YELLOW	474
	AUTUMN YELLOW	472
⑩	BRIGHT ROSE PINK	945
	BRIGHT ROSE PINK	941
⑪	GRASS GREEN	253
	GREY GREEN	351
⑫	DULL ROSE PINK	622
	BRIGHT ROSE PINK	943

TRELLIS

GRASS GREEN	256	½ hank

BACKGROUND

CHOCOLATE	181	2 hanks

BORDER

HERALDIC GOLD	843	½ hank
TURQUOISE	522	½ hank
MID BLUE	155	½ hank

METHOD

1 Find the centre of the canvas by folding in half in both directions and marking the horizontal and vertical lines with a tacking thread.
2 Following the colour code centre the pattern and work the first tree motif in tent stitch as indicated on the chart, count and work the green trellis in tent stitch around the trees and fill in the background as the work progresses.
3 When the central pattern is complete, work the outside border in gobelin, first over two threads of canvas, then two more rows over three threads of canvas.
4 To complete and make up into a cushion see the instructions on page 119.

OPPOSITE AND RIGHT A variety of colours in different combinations used with a simple pattern has produced the pretty Queen Mary's Tree Cushion

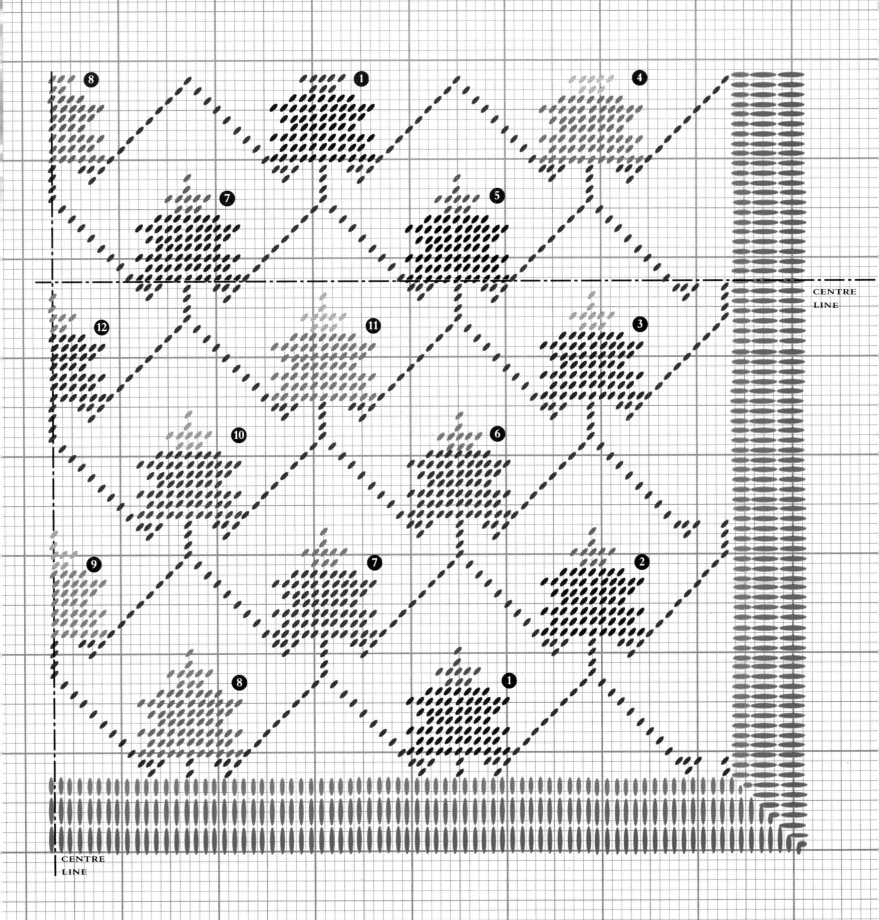

CENTRE
LINE

CENTRE
LINE

CARNATION PATTERN NEEDLECASE

Through the centuries, the carnation has been nearly as popular a motif as the strawberry. In early embroidery, flowers were associated with Christian virtues, and each had a symbolic meaning. The carnation, or dianthus (divine flower), represented love and affection and was also known as the flower of the god Zeus.

There is a pleasing feel about this motif, and the bright colours that are combined to work the pattern have resulted in a clear and attractive design. This design could be extended to any size required by adding more motifs both top and bottom, always keeping the count of the pattern correct. It is worked in tent stitch throughout. (For stitch instructions see page 124.) Each square on the chart represents one stitch on the canvas.

SIZE Needlecase 5 × 6½in (13 × 16cm) or the pattern can be adapted to fit any size

MATERIALS 9 × 10½in (23 × 27cm) mono de luxe antique canvas, 12 holes to the inch (46 holes/10cm), or no less than 4in (10cm) larger than the finished design size
Size 18 tapestry needle
Appleton tapestry wool (use one strand):

SCARLET	504	½ hank
SCARLET	502	1 skein
FLAMINGO	626	½ hank
BRIGHT PEACOCK	832	½ hank
BACKGROUND – PASTEL	877	1 hank

OPPOSITE The Carnation Needlecase uses a beautiful combination of scarlets and flamingo, with a cream background

METHOD

1 Find the centre of the canvas by folding in half in both directions and marking the horizontal and vertical lines with a tacking thread.

2 Count from the centre of the chart and start by working the first carnation nearest the centre. Work the rest of the pattern following the chart. Complete the border and then fill in the background.

3 To complete and make up the needlecase see instructions on page 120.

CENTRE LINE

CENTRE LINE

START HERE

FOLD HERE

832

626

502

504

887 *(background)*

19

Paisley Multi-coloured Repeats

This deceptively simple design is based on motifs found in paisley textiles. It is very easy to work as it uses only tent stitch throughout. I found the original pattern in an old junk shop, and realised that it would be ideal for using up those leftover pieces of wool which had accumulated in bags in every conceivable corner of my house. There are probably over 200 different colours in the example shown on the chair in the photograph.

The combination and positioning of the colours in this pattern was an exciting exercise. The blue background colour helped to link and combine the motifs, resulting in a bright and cheerful design. If this pattern is to be used for upholstering a piece of furniture, you will need to make a template (page 10). If you want to make it into a chair cover as shown, you will need to have it professionally finished. The design is worked in tent stitch throughout. (For stitch instructions see page 124.) Each square on the chart represents one stitch on the canvas.

SIZE Can be adapted to fit any size

MATERIALS Mono de luxe antique canvas, 12 holes to the inch (46 holes/10cm), no less than 4in (10cm) larger than the finished area to be upholstered

Size 18 tapestry needle

Appleton tapestry wool (use one strand):

BACKGROUND – DULL CHINA BLUE   925
PATTERN – any assorted colours

METHOD

1 Find the centre of the canvas by folding in half in both directions and marking the horizontal and vertical lines with a tacking thread.

2 If a template is being used, match the centre of the template with the centre of the canvas, making sure that all vertical and horizontal lines match and correspond with the threads of canvas. Using a bright coloured thread, sew a tacking line on the canvas around the edge of the template to mark the outline and keep the template for reference.

3 Sort out your yarns into bundles of roughly matching colours, remembering that two colours are used for each paisley shape and that the colour of each outside row should be one that will contrast with your chosen background colour so that the shape stands out.

4 Work the pattern from the centre, matching the centre point of the first paisley pattern with the centre of the canvas as indicated on the chart. Complete a small section of pattern, then fill in the background around that area, and continue working this way rather than leaving all the background until the end.

5 Work to the finish line, or match to the template tacking line or your measurements, adjusting if necessary.

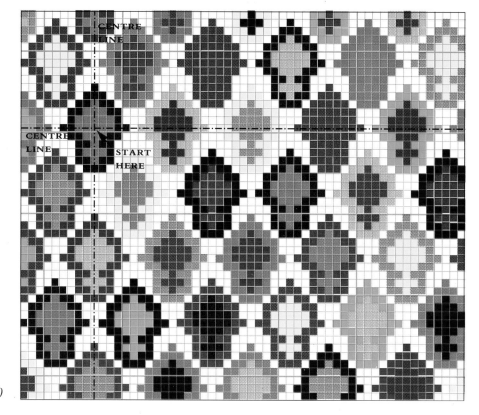

RIGHT In the Paisley Multi-coloured Repeats, the strong vibrant colours of many tapestry wools are worked together to produce a strong yet classic design, used here to upholster a chair

$\mathscr{R}$OSEBUD $\mathscr{S}$EAT $\mathscr{C}$OVER

These little rosebuds were copied from a small design found amongst some samples discovered in an old wickerwork basket a few years ago. It contained examples of every conceivable exercise in the art of darning, from the invisible mending of holes in knitwear and the patching and darning of wool blankets and sheets and sprigged cotton voiles, to the turning of hems and finishing of seams. Amongst all these exercises were samples of Berlin woolwork and repeated patterns for more leisurely sewing. However, this particular pattern has a very French feel to it, as had many other items in the box, including typically French embroidery patterns and the most wonderful sample of a Victorian woolwork French cockerel in amazingly beautiful colours.

This delightfully simple pattern is easy to work and to use as a basis for experimenting with different colours. It is a useful pattern for odd pieces of embroidery needed to fit difficult shapes. If it is used for seat covers or to uphol-ster a piece of furniture, you will need to make a template (page 10). The design is worked in cross stitch and filled in with a tent stitch background. (For stitch instructions see pages 122–124.) Each line on the chart represents one thread of canvas.

MATERIALS Mono de luxe white canvas, 12 holes to the inch (46 holes/10cm), 4in (10cm) larger than the area to be worked
Size 18 tapestry needle
For a seat cover size 13 × 13½in (33 × 34cm), I used the following quantities of **Appleton tapestry wool** (use one strand):

FLAME	202	½ hank
BRIGHT TERRACOTTA	223	½ hank
GRASS GREEN	253	½ hank
BACKGROUND		
WHITE	991	2½ hanks

METHOD

1 Find the centre of the canvas by folding in half in both directions and marking the hori-

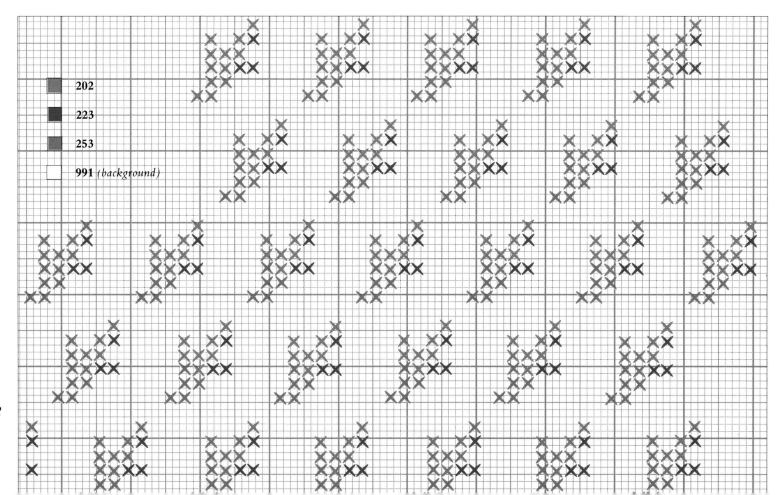

■	**202**
■	**223**
■	**253**
□	**991** *(background)*

źontal and vertical fold lines with tacking.
2 If a template is being used, match the centre of the template with the centre of the canvas, making sure that all vertical and horizontal lines match and correspond to the threads of canvas. Using a bright coloured thread, sew a tacking line on the canvas around the edge of the template to mark the outline and keep the template for reference.

3 Centre the pattern and begin the embroidery by working the rosebud motifs in cross stitch. Fill in the background in tent stitch as the work progresses.
4 Work to the finish line, or match to the template tacking line or your measurements, adjusting if necessary.
5 To complete and make up the seat cover, see instructions on page 121.

The rosebud design, with its simple cross stitches, makes an ideal chair seat cover

Sprigged Rose Tiebacks

This pretty rose pattern worked in tent stitch was discovered amongst some old samples given to me several years ago. The clever placing of the roses across the canvas gives a pleasing effect and it would be a useful small repeating motif for a chair seat, tieback or footstool in a room where a lot of pattern has already been used.

Worked here in pastel colours to give a soft and subtle look, the design would work just as well in stronger colours using a dark background colour. The design is worked in tent stitch throughout. (For stitch instructions see page 124.) Each square on the chart represents one stitch on the canvas.

SIZE Each tieback is 23½in (60cm) long and 4in (10cm) wide or the pattern can be used for any size

MATERIALS 28½ × 8in (72 × 20cm) mono de luxe white canvas, 12 holes to the inch (46 holes/10cm), or a piece of canvas 4in (10cm) larger than the area to be worked for each tieback

Size 18 tapestry needle

Appleton tapestry wool (use one strand):

ROSE PINK	752	½ hank
ROSE PINK	754	¾ hank
ROSE PINK	756	¼ hank
GREY GREEN	355	¾ hank
BACKGROUND		
WHITE	991	2 hanks

METHOD

1 Find the centre of the canvas by folding in half in both directions and marking the horizontal and vertical lines with a tacking thread.

2 Start by working the centre rose flower in tent stitch as indicated on the chart, making sure the pattern is correctly positioned with an allowance made for the turnings.

3 Fill in the background as the work progresses.

4 To complete and make up the tiebacks see instructions on page 120.

OPPOSITE The Sprigged Rose Tiebacks use a simple pattern, worked across the canvas in tent stitch

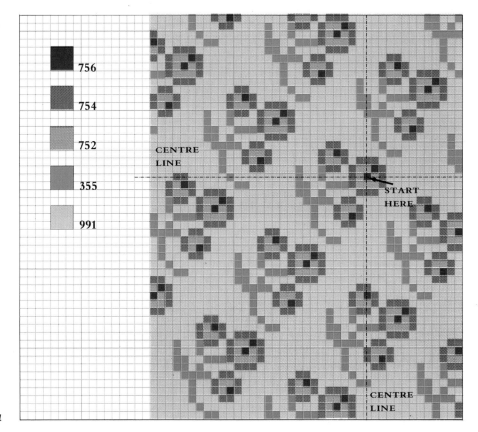

756

754

752

355

991

CENTRE LINE

START HERE

CENTRE LINE

Patchwork Blocks

Reminiscent of the shapes used in patchwork, this simple pattern is worked in tent stitch and would be easy for a beginner. The vivid colours of the patchwork blocks have been subdued by a brown background, while the thoughtful placing of these combinations has produced an exciting mix. The design would work equally well using any other bright colour combination. Pale pastel colours would give a soft muted look, and a different textured finish could be achieved by using stranded cotton in the centre of each block.

If this pattern is used for a footstool cover or to upholster a piece of furniture, you will need to make a template (page 10). The design is worked in tent stitch throughout. (For stitch instructions see page 124.) Each square on the chart represents one stitch on the canvas.

SIZE Can be adapted to fit any size

MATERIALS Mono de luxe antique canvas, 12 holes to the inch (46 holes/10cm), 4in (10cm) larger than the area to be worked
Size 18 tapestry needle

Appleton tapestry wool (use one strand):

BACKGROUND

BROWN GROUNDING	581

Suggested colour combinations:

{ ROSE PINK	755
{ ROSE PINK	757
{ BRIGHT CHINA BLUE	744
{ ROYAL BLUE	822
{ EARLY ENGLISH GREEN	544
{ EARLY ENGLISH GREEN	546
{ HERALDIC GOLD	842
{ HERALDIC GOLD	844
CENTRES	
WHITE	992

METHOD

1 Find the centre of the canvas by folding in half in both directions and marking the horizontal and vertical lines with a tacking thread.

2 If a template is used, match the centre of the template to the centre of the canvas, making sure that all vertical and horizontal lines match and correspond with the threads of canvas.

3 Using a bright coloured thread, sew a tacking line on the canvas around the edge of the template to mark the outline and keep the template for reference.

4 Centre the pattern and start by working the brown outline to each diamond.

5 Fill in each pattern with the relative colours before moving on to the next area.

6 Only work one colour at a time to avoid tangling threads on the back of the work.

7 Work to the finish line, or match to the template tacking line or your measurements, adjusting if necessary.

OPPOSITE The diamonds of the Patchwork Blocks design have been worked in bright jewel colours to upholster this footstool

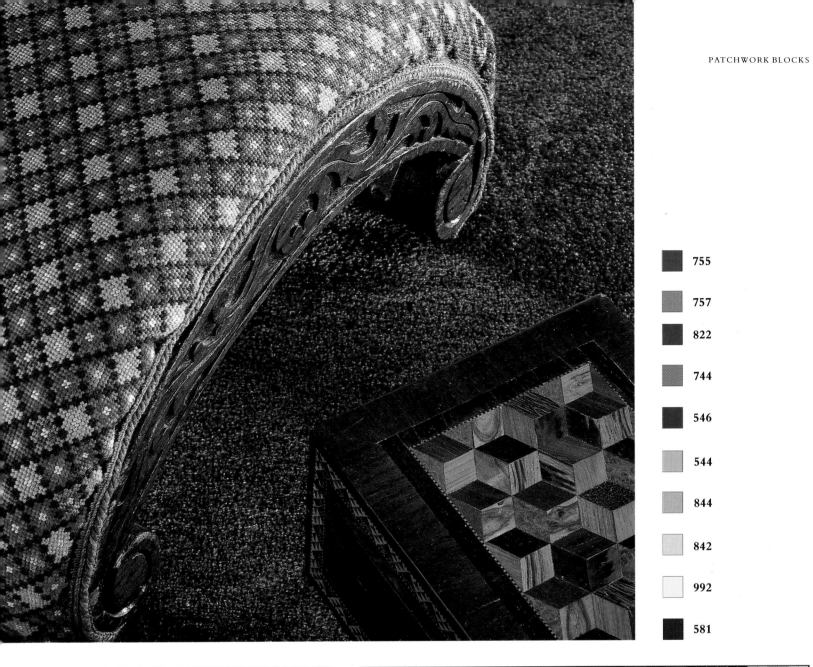

	755
	757
	822
	744
	546
	544
	844
	842
	992
	581

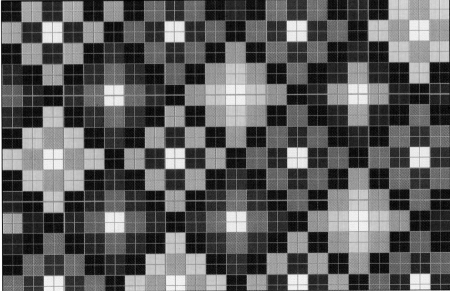

Chapter Two

Samplers

*T*HE MAKING of samplers is an ancient craft. Even the very earliest known examples, found in Egyptian burial tombs, show different patterns, stitches and techniques worked on fabric.

Before pattern books were available, samplers were the only means of recording stitches and patterns. They were used by beginners as a learning aid and reference to show how the stitches were worked; then they would be copied as a means of practising the stitches. Inspiration for the designs came from woodcuts, illustrated manuscripts or even herbals and the threads were silks and fine wools dyed naturally.

By the middle of the sixteenth century, domestic embroidery was growing in popularity and was used extensively to decorate household linens and furnishings, while clothes were richly embroidered and trimmed with beautiful laces. Needlework would occupy the greater part of a lady's day and was a way of life in upperclass households. Making samplers was an easy way of recording new patterns so that they could be used again later and passed on to other people. Towards the end of the century, pattern books were being produced commercially and the popular patterns which appeared in many different samplers of this period can be traced back to these.

A book first published in 1624, titled A Shole-house for the Needle by Richard Shorleyker, contained many small motifs of fruit, birds, fish and flowers. Lace patterns with details of other

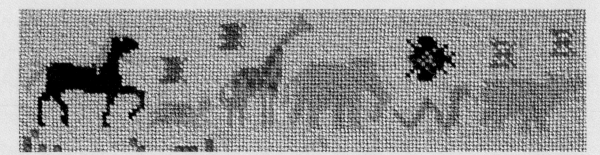

embroidery were also included. Many of the small motifs from this book have survived, have been adapted, and are still in use today.

The eighteenth-century samplers showed less reliance on the old printed books, and the fashion for more natural types of flower designs, found on the printed textiles of that period, were interpreted onto samplers. Pattern books became expensive and professionally drawn samplers became a cheaper way of producing these designs; the outline of the pattern would be drawn onto the fabric ready for working (rather like our printed designs today). Map samplers, showing different counties, were worked in the same way. Many of those which have survived were obviously commercially produced, as they are identical except for the occasional small personal touch such as a pretty flower border, the stitcher's name, and perhaps the place where they lived marked on the map in the appropriate place.

Commercially produced printed patterns on linen and canvas became popular in the nineteenth century, and there was also an increase in the production of pattern books with detailed instructions, so samplers were no longer necessary to record techniques and patterns. At this time Berlin woolwork became very fashionable, worked from hand-coloured or printed charts on squared paper. Samplers were, however, still being made by the Victorians, possibly to make confusing or badly coloured charts easier to understand and copy.

Today, interest in samplers has seen something of a revival. Antique needlework samplers have become collectors' items and are difficult to find and expensive to buy, but they are a wonderful source of ideas for new designs. A sampler is fun to sew, makes a popular gift and looks very decorative framed and hung on the wall.

Alphabet Sampler

Working a sampler was an essential part of a Victorian girl's education, as it would teach her techniques and stitches that would be useful after her marriage to decorate both her home and her clothes. Embroidery was also a leisure pursuit for ladies, who had plenty of time for such work, especially as servants did the mending and plain sewing and dressmakers made their clothes.

This design is typical of the Berlin woolwork samplers of the Victorian era, which would have a border of little rosebuds or carnations, spot motifs, a pious verse and an alphabet with the date and age of the child working it. The finished sampler would then be framed and hung on the wall by the proud parents. The delightfully simple alphabet has a typical rosebud border and rosebuds intertwining through the letters. It could be made into a cushion or framed as a picture.

This design uses only tent stitch, so would be suitable for a beginner to work. (For stitch instructions see page 124.) Each square on the chart represents one stitch.

SIZE 15½ × 12½in (39 × 32cm)

MATERIALS 20 × 17in (51 × 43cm) mono de luxe antique canvas, 14 holes to the inch (56 holes/10cm)
Size 20 tapestry needle
Appleton crewel wool (use three strands):

ROSE PINK	752	¼ hank
ROSE PINK	754	¼ hank
HERALDIC GOLD	841	¾ hank
PASTEL	874	¼ hank
SEA GREEN	402	½ hank
BACKGROUND		
BRIGHT PEACOCK	835	3 hanks

METHOD

1 Find the centre of the canvas by folding in half in both directions and marking the horizontal and vertical lines with a tacking thread.
2 Following the colour code and counting the stitches from the chart onto the canvas, start in the centre. Work the letters first, using tent stitch, filling in the background as work progresses, also using tent stitch.
3 To work the border, start from the centre line and work the first flower shown on the chart, then complete the remainder of the border.

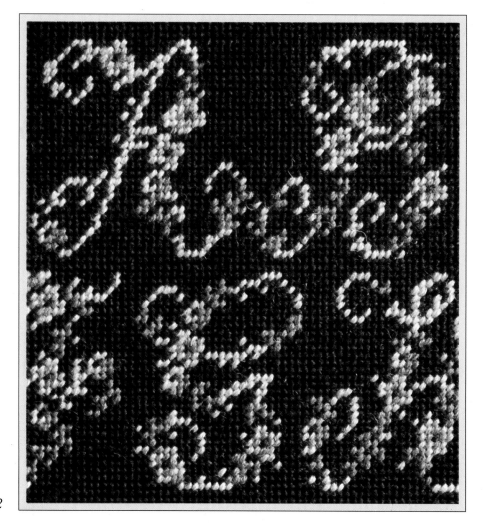

RIGHT The classic Alphabet Sampler combines roses with letters from a traditional alphabet, all worked in one simple stitch

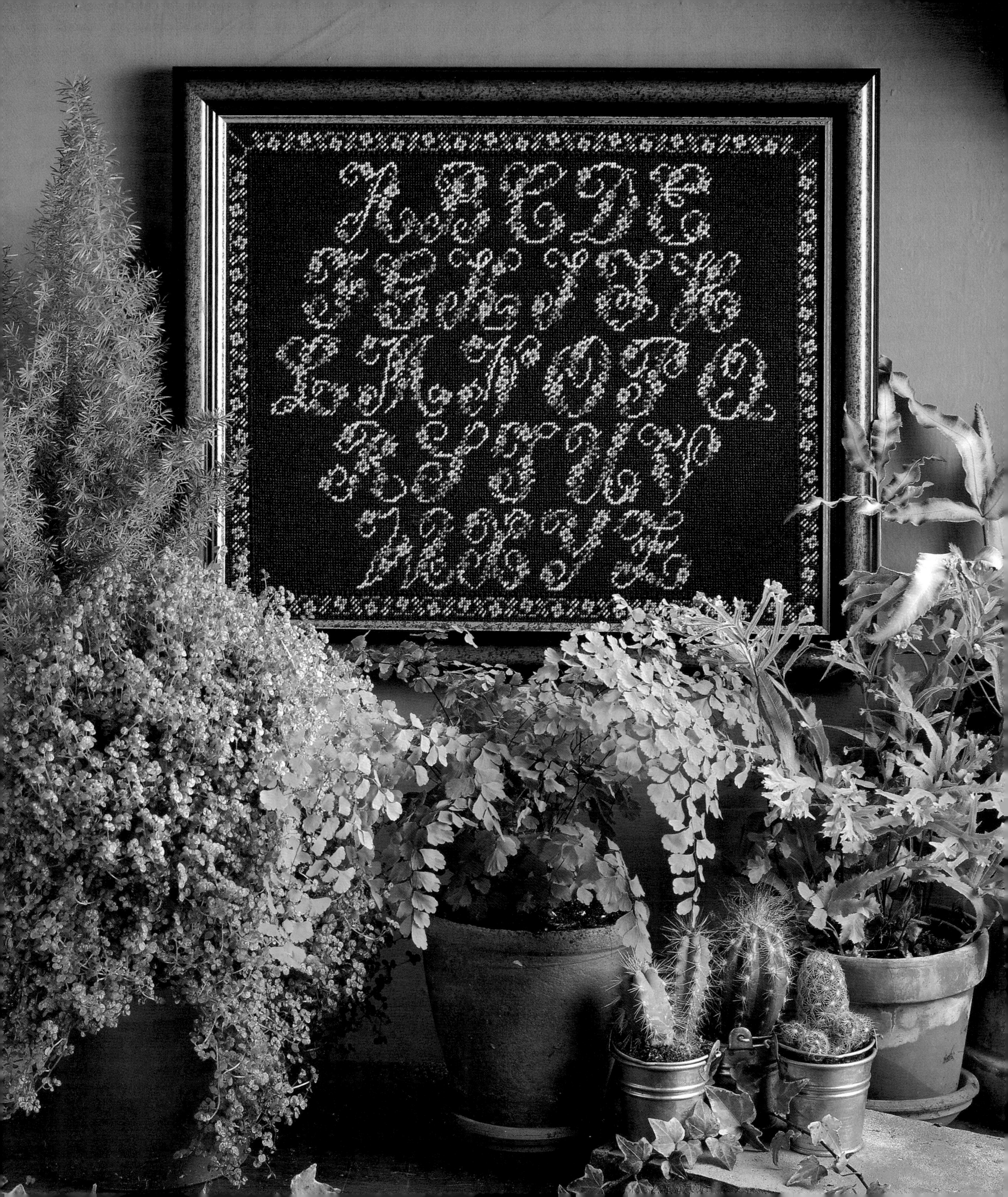
ABCDE
FGHIJK
LMNOPQ
RSTUV
WXYZ

754

752

402

874

841

835 *(background)*

CENTRE LINE

START
BORDER
HERE

...And the Animals

The story of Noah and his animals is the theme of this sampler, which has been designed with a child's room in mind. The positioning of the animals around the border and the traditional lettering in the centre make a pleasing picture to hang on the wall of a playroom or nursery. The sampler could be adapted to give a child's name and date of birth instead of the numbers, whilst a longer message could replace the alphabet.

This design uses four easy textured stitches: tent, cross, and straight and slanting gobelin, so it would be suitable for a beginner to work. (For stitch instructions see pages 122–124.) Each line on the chart represents one thread of canvas.

. . . And the Animals, with its amusing depiction of Noah and the Ark, would be fun to work as a gift for a child

SIZE 10½ × 14½in (27 × 37cm)

MATERIALS 15 × 19in (38 × 48cm) mono de luxe antique canvas, 14 holes to the inch (56 holes/10cm)
Graph paper large enough to work out your chosen initials
Size 20 tapestry needle
Appleton crewel wool (use three strands throughout):

ROSE PINK	751	1 skein
BRIGHT TERRACOTTA	224	¼ hank
BRIGHT CHINA BLUE	745	1 skein
IRON GREY	963	¼ hank
SEA GREEN	402	¼ hank
HONEYSUCKLE	695	1 skein
HONEYSUCKLE	698	1 skein
BROWN GROUNDING	586	½ hank
WHITE	991	¼ hank
BACKGROUND		
HONEYSUCKLE	691	2½ hanks

METHOD

1 Find the centre of the canvas by folding in half in both directions and marking the horizontal and vertical fold lines with a tacking thread.

2 Following the colour code and counting the stitches from the chart onto the canvas, start in the centre. Work all the alphabet letters, using cross stitch, filling in the background with tent stitch as work progresses.

3 Next, work the boat below the letters using tent, slanting gobelin and cross stitch, then work the waves in cross stitch and the numbers in tent stitch before filling in the background around them with tent stitch.

4 The entire animal border is worked in tent stitch. Start from the horizontal centre line and work the first elephant. Then continue working to complete all the animals following the colour code and counting the stitches onto the canvas from the chart.

5 Complete the design by filling in the background around the border.

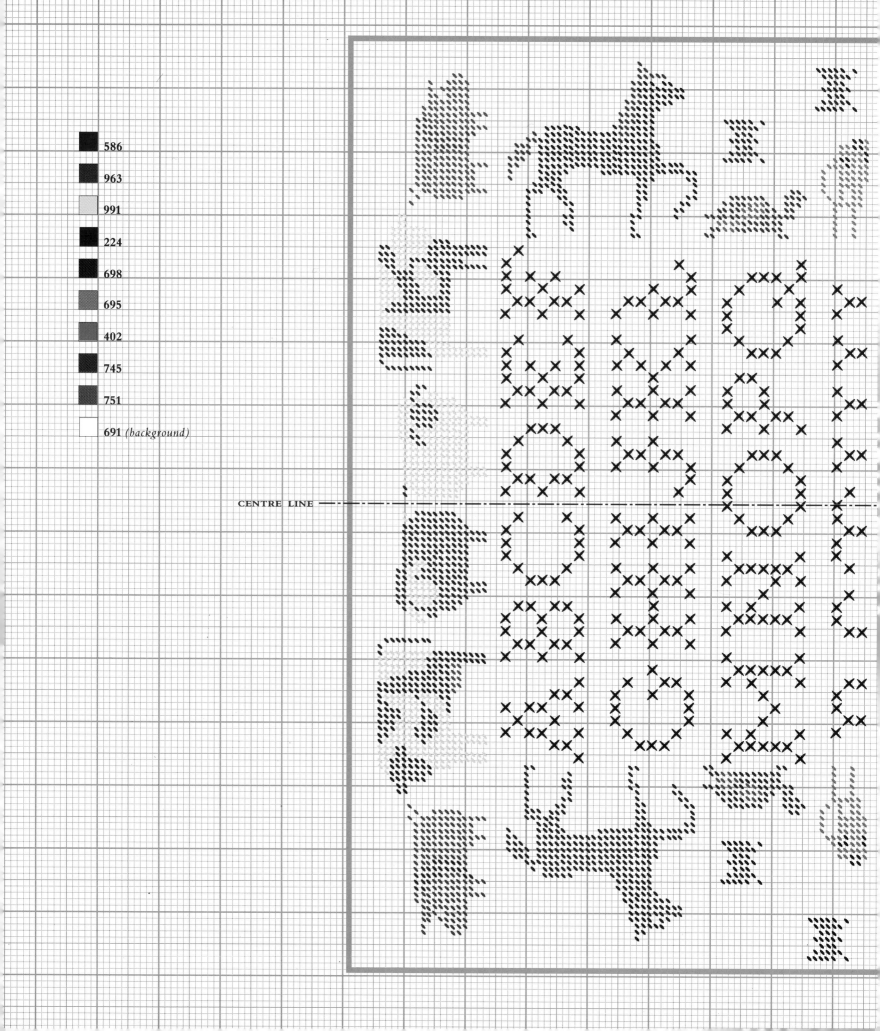

586

963

991

224

698

695

402

745

751

691 *(background)*

CENTRE LINE

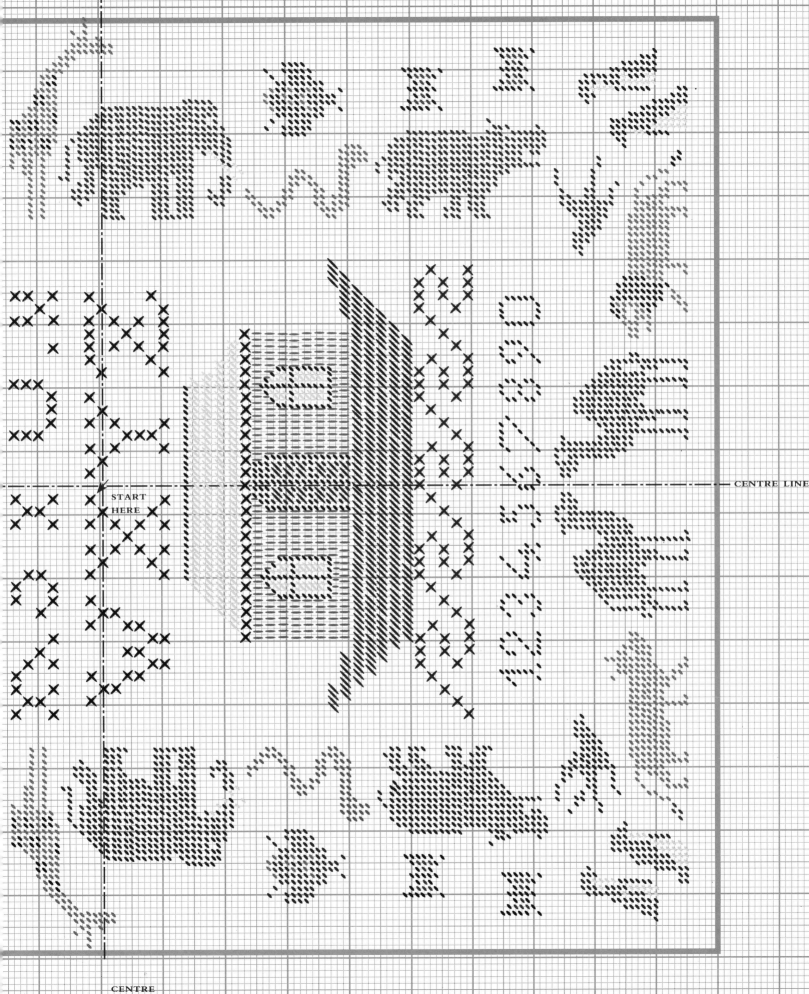

CENTRE LINE

START
HERE

CENTRE
LINE

Victorian Cross Stitch Sampler

Berlin woolwork was a very distinctive sewing fashion of the Victorian era. Designs were worked from charts using wools imported from Germany and girls from upper-class families were taught at home, working their samplers under the strict eye of a governess. The popular samplers often had alphabets and numbers in cross stitch, with little motifs of birds, animals and flowers. (Many such designs could also be used in tiny stitches to mark linen.) Girls were also instructed in all the techniques for making and mending clothes, and many worked samplers of minute proportions to practise the necessary neatness and precision.

The double canvas used for this sampler would be typical of the canvas used in the latter part of the nineteenth century, and the colours capture the feel and style of Berlin woolwork with a traditional unworked background.

This sampler uses only cross stitch, in one strand of crewel wool throughout. The background has not been filled in but could be worked with tent stitch (3 strands). (For stitch instructions see pages 122–124.) Each square on the chart represents one stitch on the canvas.

SIZE 23¾ × 17½in (60 × 44cm)

MATERIALS 28 × 22in (70 × 55cm) double-thread antique-brown canvas, 12 holes to the inch (46 holes/10cm)

Graph paper large enough to work out your chosen initials

Size 20 tapestry needle

Appleton crewel wool (use one strand throughout):

AUTUMN YELLOW	472	½ hank
AUTUMN YELLOW	475	¼ hank
AUTUMN YELLOW	478	¼ hank
ROSE PINK	754	½ hank
ROSE PINK	756	½ hank
EARLY ENGLISH GREEN	542	½ hank
EARLY ENGLISH GREEN	544	1½ hanks
EARLY ENGLISH GREEN	545	2½ hanks

OPPOSITE The Victorian Cross Stitch Sampler captures the feel and style of Berlin woolwork

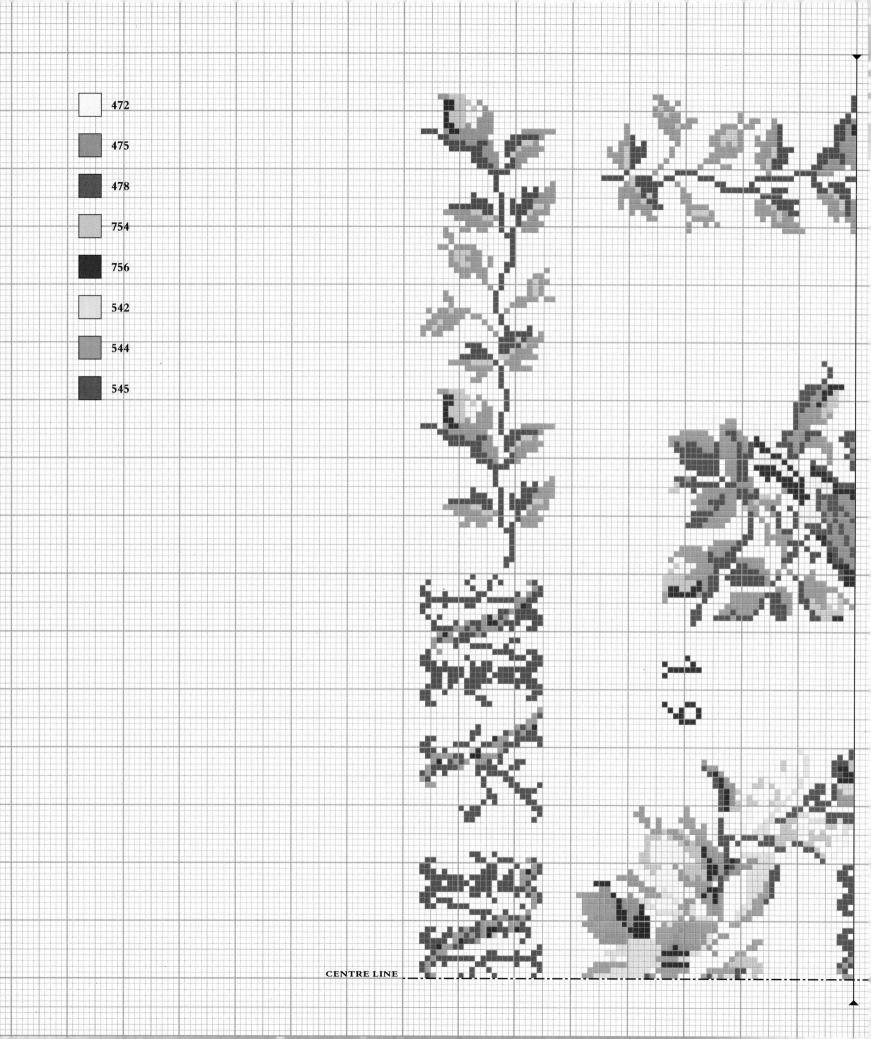

472

475

478

754

756

542

544

545

CENTRE LINE

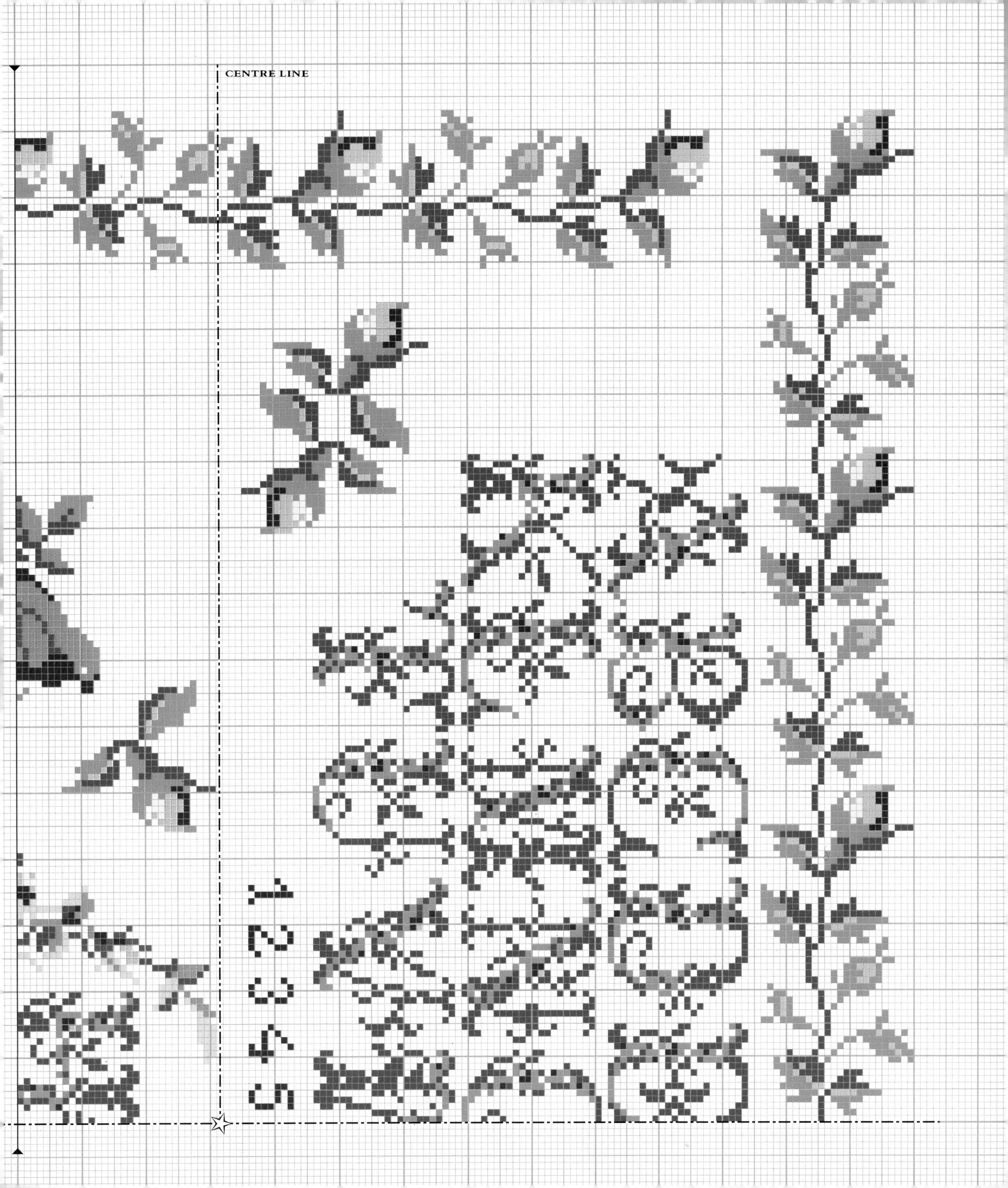
CENTRE LINE

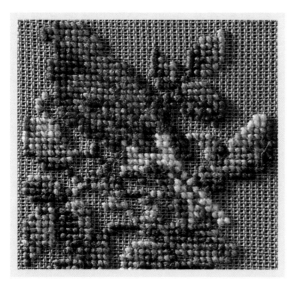

METHOD

1 Find the centre of the canvas by folding in half in both directions and marking the horizontal and vertical lines with a tacking thread.

2 Following the colour code and counting the stitches from the chart onto the canvas, start in the centre, working the first leaf of the central garland. Because the background of this sampler is unworked, it is important not to have any trailing threads which would show through when the sampler is made up or framed. All starting and finishing threads should be darned into the back of previously worked stitches, and all thread ends should be trimmed very short to keep the back of the embroidery as neat as possible.

3 Work the central motif and the birds on each side, omitting the initials, then work the remaining motifs and the alphabet.

4 To work the chosen initials in the central motif, you will need a piece of graph paper, pencil and eraser. Count the spaces to be filled onto the graph paper and mark the area, then count the letters to be used and centre them on the marked area of the graph paper. When they are correctly centred, work them on the canvas using the colours from the colour key.

5 To work the border, start from the centre line, following the colour code and counting the stitches on to the canvas from the chart.

CENTRE

START HERE

CENTRE LINE

House and Garden Sampler

The most traditional sampler images are used in this design of a country house set in gardens with countryside in the background, and surrounded by a border of strawberries. Samplers would very often tell a story and portray an embroidered stately home with family crests and household pets. Sometimes real people would appear amongst the rows of classic borders and patterns, making very personal mementoes to be kept and passed down through the family.

Many of these samplers were divided into three. In the top section would be a pious verse or alphabet, in the middle a house or scene, then at the bottom a garden with animals, birds and butterflies. The sections would be divided by two decorative borders and the whole sampler would be framed with a traditional floral border. A variety of stitches and different techniques would probably be incorporated into the design.

This sampler could be adapted to include dates and initials or even a message. There is space at the top in the sky at each side of the house for initials and dates, or a longer message could be worked where the alphabet is shown. This sampler uses seven textured stitches: tent, cross, leaf, brick, Scottish variation, straight gobelin and Hungarian variation. Because so many different stitches are used, it may be more difficult for a beginner to work. (For stitch instructions see pages 122–124.) Each line on the chart represents one thread of canvas.

SIZE 14½ × 12in (37 × 30cm)

MATERIALS 19 × 16in (47 × 40cm) mono de luxe antique canvas, 14 holes to the inch (56 holes/10cm)

Graph paper large enough to work out your chosen words, initials or dates to replace alphabet and numbers, if required

Size 20 tapestry needle

Appleton crewel wool (use three strands throughout):

BRIGHT CHINA BLUE	743	½ hank
HONEYSUCKLE	695	¼ hank
EARLY ENGLISH GREEN	543	½ hank
EARLY ENGLISH GREEN	545	½ hank
WHITE	991	¼ hank
BRIGHT TERRACOTTA	224	¾ hank
BACKGROUND		
HONEYSUCKLE	691	2¾ hanks

METHOD

1 Find the centre of the canvas by folding in half in both directions and marking the horizontal and vertical lines with a tacking thread.

2 Counting the stitches from the chart onto the canvas, and using the colours according to the colour code, stitch the path up to the house first, starting at the centre point.

3 Next, work the trees and birds on either side of the house and fill in the background in tent stitch as work progresses. Fill in the sky around the house followed by the path either side of the house. Work the fence, then the flowerbeds.

4 Finally complete the alphabet, filling in the background as you work.

5 To work the border, start from the centre line following the colour code and counting the stitches onto the canvas from the chart, starting with a cross stitch. Complete the strawberries and leaves, filling in the background in tent stitch as work progresses.

The traditional House and Garden Sampler could become a cherished family heirloom

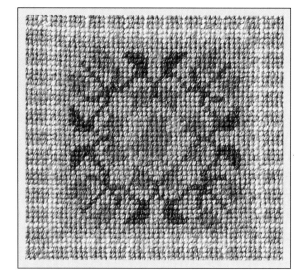

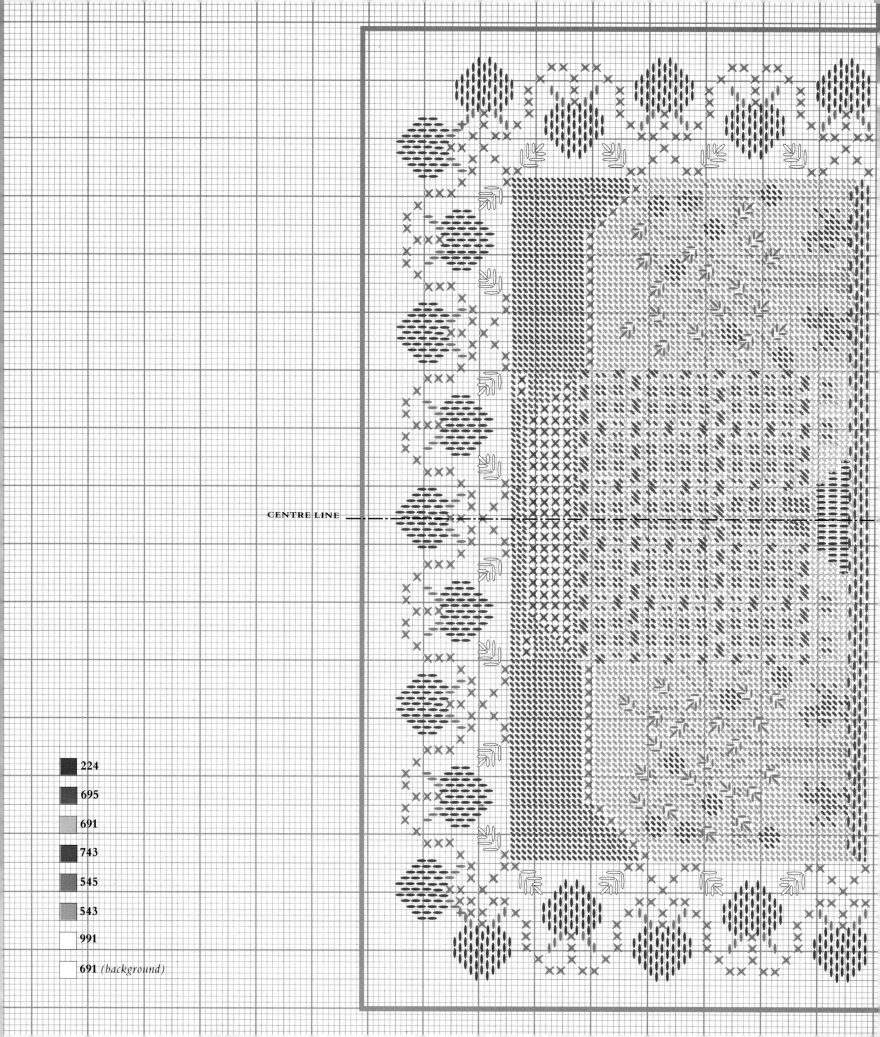

CENTRE LINE

224

695

691

743

545

543

991

691 (background)

CENTRE
START
HERE

CENTRE LINE

Chapter Three

BEADWORK

*T*HE DECORATION *of jewellery and textiles with beads is a skill which has been used throughout the world for many hundreds of years. In the Middle East, beadwork was developed into a fine craft, and in medieval times, beads were exported by glassmaking countries such as Italy and France. Elizabethan court portraits show how beads were used in the fifteenth century. Semi-precious stones and seed pearls which may have come from British river beds were expertly sewn on to courtiers' elaborate clothes and enhanced by highly skilful gold thread embroidery worked on luxury fabrics, using especially fine needles. The poorer people would have imitated these grand clothes, substituting glass, bone and wood beads on their much coarser materials.*

In the seventeenth century, bead embroidery was used to cover objects like caskets, jewel boxes, belts and purses completely, as well as being used to decorate textiles. During this period all forms of embroidery were very much a part of a girl's education, and beadwork techniques were the last stage in this education. A young girl might also be instructed to work a jewel casket with bead-embroidered panels and lid; very often the patterns and images used on these would be the same as those used on other types of embroidery, as they were frequently taken from the same design books and prints.

As fashions changed, so did the use of beads. Throughout the eighteenth century increasingly lighter fabrics were used and, as they could not be so heavily beaded, the use of beads became simpler. About the same time, smaller, more intricate items, such as watch chains, needlecases and napkin rings, were covered in beads.

It is fairly easy to date a piece of bead embroidery by the size of the beads, as they tended to get larger towards the end of the nineteenth century. There were several different methods for applying beads, either on a loom, using a tambour frame, or with a needle and thread.

The Victorian era saw a revival of interest in handcrafts and as this grew so did the availability of new patterns and supplies. Many magazines published clear embroidery patterns which could be used to combine Victorian woolwork with beads. Sometimes the beads would highlight the design, or the whole pattern might be worked entirely in beads, leaving the background to be worked in yarn or stranded cotton. As far as the Victorians were concerned, all manner of household and personal belongings could be decorated with beads: teapot stands, firescreens, pelmets, mantelpiece covers, mats, belts, braces, hats and cushions. Towards the end of the nineteenth century, beads were again used extensively to decorate clothes, from day wear to ballgowns, while jet beads were used to enhance mourning clothes.

During the early part of the twentieth century there was little interest in beading, until the Twenties, when beaded cocktail dresses and accessories such as shoes, handbags and hats became fashionable. Many of these articles have survived and are in family collections.

In this chapter, only one type of bead is used, on a double canvas (stitched with a fine needle and thread). The beads are available from specialist needlework and craft shops. The double canvas is strong enough to hold the beads in place and forms a good base for a background worked in crewel wool. Each bead will lie on the canvas in the opposite direction to the tent stitch background. To prevent twisting threads and to strengthen the yarn, cover the cotton thread with wax using a beeswax tablet available from specialist needlework shops. Tent stitch is used to work the background areas. Cross stitch and other textured stitches may be used to frame the design.

BEADED TUDOR CUSHION

Inspired by images from Tudor and Elizabethan embroideries, this bead-work cushion depicts flowers and insects in beads within a gold frame-work. Sixteenth-century bead embroidery was elaborate and used the finest beads, often made of semi-precious stones and pearls, which were so tiny it is difficult to imagine how they were threaded and sewn onto the fabric. Glass beads imported from Europe were often used on caskets and in embroidered pictures showing Biblical scenes. These scenes were often exquisite collections of small and large animals, insects, castles, rivers and hillocks, frequently out of proportion.

This small cushion is easy to make and uses lots of different coloured beads with gold metallic thread. The beads are applied onto the design with a diagonal stitch over two close threads of canvas; the background is filled in with tent stitch using three strands of crewel wool over two close threads of canvas. (For beading and stitch instructions see pages 122–124.) Each line on the chart represents two close threads of canvas.

SIZE 13 × 9in (33 × 23cm)

MATERIALS 17 × 13in (43 × 33cm) double-thread antique canvas, 12 holes to the inch (46 holes/10cm)
Size 9 straw needle for beading
Size 20 tapestry needle
Appleton crewel wool: Cornflower 465, 2 hanks (use three strands)
Cotton sewing thread for applying beads
Madeira Gold metallic thread No 8, colour 8013, 3 reels

The richly beaded Tudor Cushion depicting flowers and insects was inspired by embroideries of the sixteenth century

Mill Hill Glass Seed Beads:

CHRISTMAS GREEN	167	3 packs
CHRISTMAS RED	165	3 packs
RAINBOW	374	1 pack
MERCURY	283	1 pack
COBALT BLUE	358	1 pack
VIOLET	206	1 pack
IRIS	252	1 pack
SAPPHIRE	168	1 pack
PINK	145	1 pack
TEA ROSE	2004	1 pack
YELLOW CREAM	2002	1 pack
YELLOW	128	1 pack
SAPPHIRE	168	1 pack
PINK	145	1 pack
RED	968	1 pack
VICTORIAN GOLD	2011	1 pack
EMERALD	332	1 pack
ICE LILAC	2009	1 pack
ROBINS EGG BLUE	143	1 pack
SATIN BLUE	2007	1 pack
WHITE	479	1 pack

METHOD

1 Find the centre of the canvas by folding in half in both directions and marking the horizontal and vertical lines with a tacking thread.

2 Start at the centre of the chart by working the diamond framework pattern in gold thread, working from the centre outwards. Thread the tapestry needle with a short length of gold thread about 14in (36cm) long; a longer length will fray. Work in cross stitch to complete frames and border before starting the beadwork.

3 Thread the straw needle with a doubled cotton or similar sewing thread and apply the beads, working from the chart to fill the frames with the patterns. The beads will lie in the opposite direction to the tent stitch background.

4 Thread the tapestry needle with three strands of wool and work the background in tent stitch over two close threads of canvas to the finish line.

5 To make up the cushion, see the instructions on page 119.

8013 *(gold thread)*

2011

167

165

479

128

2009

143

2007

283

2004

145

374

252

2002

206

168

332

358

968

465 *(background thread)*

START HERE

CENTRE LINE

CENTRE LINE

Beaded Floral Wreath Footstool

A traditional combination of
intertwining flowers and
leaves embroidered with
beads. The finished design,
used here to upholster a
Victorian-style inlaid
mahogany footstool, could
also be used to make a cushion

58

MATERIALS 17in sq (43cm sq) double-thread antique canvas, 12 holes to the inch (46 holes/10cm)

Size 9 straw needle for beading

Size 20 tapestry needle

Appleton crewel wool: Brown Grounding 585, 3 hanks (use three strands)

Cotton sewing thread for applying beads

Mill Hill Glass Seed Beads:

CHRISTMAS GREEN	167	5 packs
MERCURY	283	4 packs
PINK	451	1 pack
TEA ROSE	2004	2 packs
RED	968	1 pack
LIGHT BLUE	146	1 pack
SAPPHIRE	168	1 pack
IRIS	252	1 pack
WHITE	479	1 pack
TANGERINE	423	1 pack
GARNET	367	1 pack
ASH MAUVE	151	1 pack
ICE LILAC	2009	1 pack
YELLOW	128	1 pack

This pretty wreath of flowers worked in beads has been designed to fit a round footstool, but could equally be made into a square for a cushion. The design was inspired by Berlin woolwork patterns which were fashionable throughout the nineteenth century. The beading of these patterns became very popular in the middle of the century, using delicately coloured beads imported from France. Some designs were very effectively worked in shades of black, grey and white beads.

This pattern is worked with beads which are applied onto the design with a diagonal stitch over two close threads of canvas; the background is filled in with tent stitch using three strands of crewel wool over two close threads of canvas. (For beading and stitch instructions, see page 124.) Each square on the chart represents one bead or one tent stitch of the background.

SIZE Finished design size 12½in (32cm)

NOTE: This design can be extended by increasing the background area to fit a larger footstool or could be made into a square for an upholstered cushion.

METHOD

1 Find the centre of the canvas by folding in half in both directions and marking the horizontal and vertical lines with a tacking thread. Draw a circle from the centre of the canvas to the required size for your footstool using a pencil and then tack round the pencil line.

2 Find the centre of the chart and count on the canvas to the first flower to be worked.

3 Thread the straw needle with cotton or similar sewing thread and, using a double thread, apply the beads, working from the first flower. Sew all the beaded parts of the design following the coloured beading chart. The beads will lie in the opposite direction to the tent stitch background.

4 Thread the larger tapestry needle with three strands of wool and work the background to the finish circle line.

5 To mount onto a footstool or make up as a cushion see pages 119 and 121.

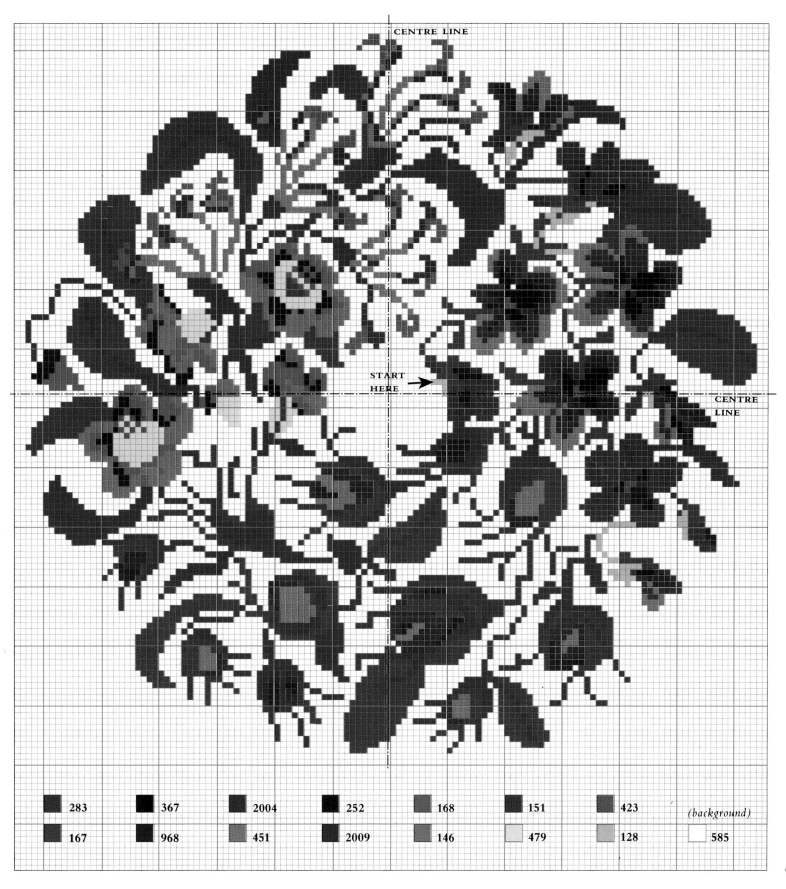

CENTRE LINE

START
HERE

CENTRE
LINE

| | 283 | | 367 | | 2004 | | 252 | | 168 | | 151 | | 423 | | | (background) |
| | 167 | | 968 | | 451 | | 2009 | | 146 | | 479 | | 128 | | | 585 |

Beaded Rosebud Waistcoat

The design of this waistcoat was influenced by silk embroideries of the seventeenth century. Many fine embroidered waistcoats are still in beautiful condition, both in private and public collections, which suggests that they were highly valued and well looked after. I have even seen one or two unfinished waistcoats still wrapped in tissue paper; these provide us with valuable clues about how waistcoats of the period were constructed.

These seventeenth-century waistcoats were embroidered heavily around the edges, with a spot motif worked all over the background. Here and there the pattern would be enhanced by coiled metal threads and small steel sequins, and very often both the pocket flaps and buttons were worked in the same pattern. Very well-made, fine needles must have been essential for such fine work.

This waistcoat features flowers and leaves which intertwine around each other as they might grow in a garden. Both the look and feel of this type of design echo textiles and embroideries of the seventeenth century, which were often inspired by oriental patterns.

This pattern is worked with beads which are applied onto the design with a diagonal stitch over two close threads of canvas and the background is filled in with tent stitch using three strands of crewel wool over two close threads of canvas.

This project is for reasonably experienced embroiderers and dressmakers. The waistcoat itself was made from a commercial paper pattern which is widely available and can be adjusted to fit other sizes. (For beading and tent stitch instructions see page 124.) Each square on the canvas represents one bead or one tent stitch of the background.

SIZE To fit medium chest size 36–38in (92–97cm). The size of the waistcoat may be altered and the design of the beaded embroidery adjusted accordingly.

MATERIALS 28×35in (70×90cm) double-thread antique canvas, 12 holes to the inch (46 holes/10cm)
Size 9 straw needle for beading
Size 20 tapestry needle
Appleton crewel wool: Rose Pink 759, 8 hanks (use three strands)
Cotton sewing thread for applying beads
Mill Hill Glass Seed Beads:

RED	968	4 packs
CHRISTMAS GREEN	167	11 packs

METHOD

1 Centre the two fronts of the paper pattern on the canvas and pin and tack around the outer edge to mark the outline. If the pattern has darts, do not mark them as they would be too bulky on the finished design but compensate by taking ¼in (5mm) out of the side seams.

2 Remove the paper pattern and work an inner row of tacking to show the seam allowances which will be left unworked.

3 Cut the canvas in half so that each front is a separate piece. Do not cut round the edge but leave each half as a rectangular piece of canvas so that it can be attached to a frame if necessary.

4 To mark the centre of each waistcoat front, fold the canvas in half in both directions and mark the horizontal and vertical lines with tacking.

5 Find the centre of the chart and count to the outside edge of the canvas to start the first beaded flower.

6 Thread the straw needle with a doubled cotton or similar thread and apply the beads, working from the first flower. Sew all the beaded areas of the design, following the coloured beading chart. The beads will lie in the opposite direction to the tent stitch background.

7 Thread the larger tapestry needle with three strands of wool and work the background to the inner row of tacking thread, leaving the seam allowances unworked.

8 Complete both sides of the waistcoat front.

9 Make up following the step-by-step instructions supplied with the paper pattern.

OPPOSITE The look and feel of the Rosebud Waistcoat echo textiles and embroideries of the seventeenth century

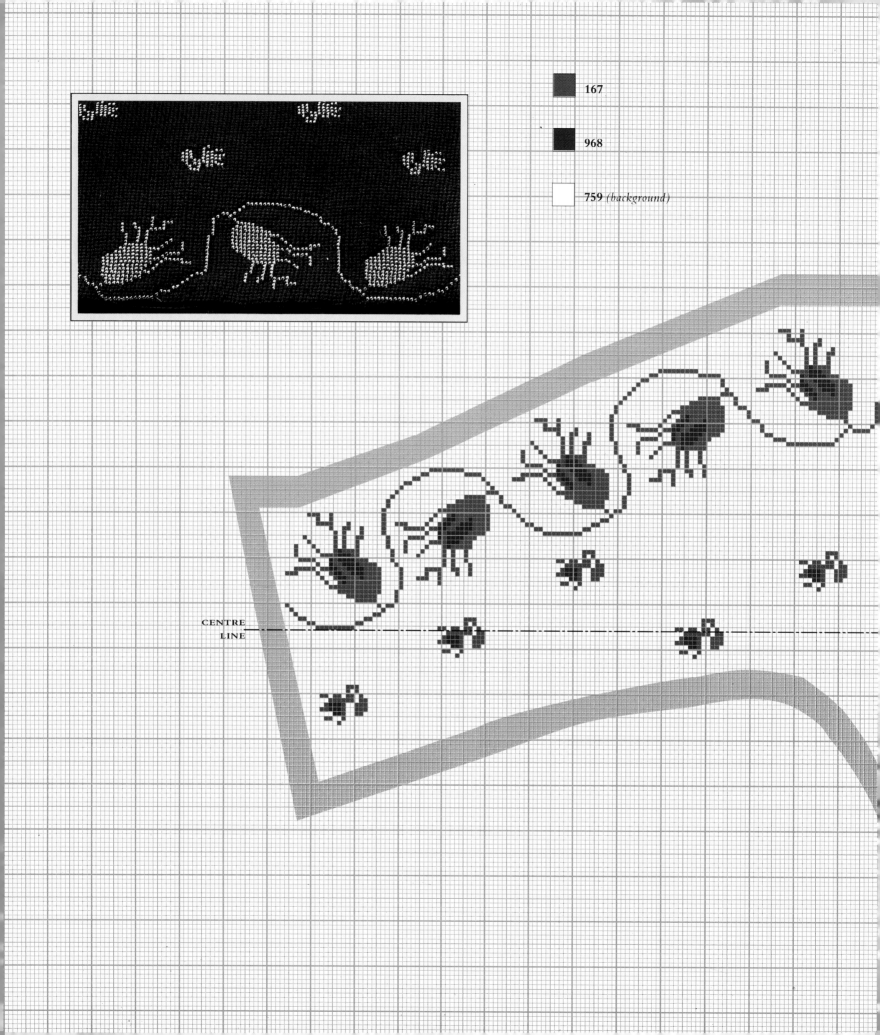

167

968

759 *(background)*

CENTRE
LINE

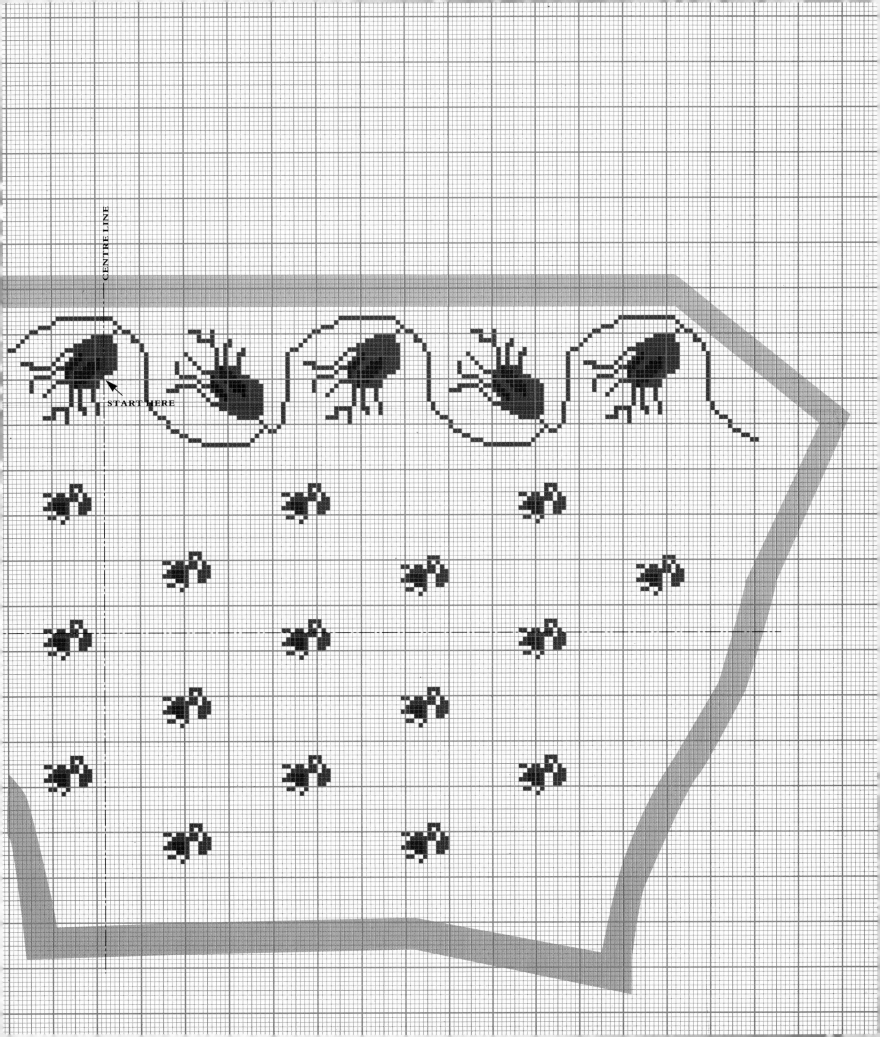

CENTRE LINE

START HERE

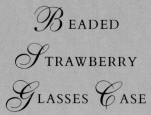

*B*EADED
*S*TRAWBERRY
*G*LASSES *C*ASE

The beads on the Strawberry Glasses Case reflect the glowing colour of real strawberries

The strawberry motif appears through the centuries in all forms of embroidery, particularly samplers – equalled in popularity only by the carnation. Early designs showing the entire plant occur in the background of paintings, sewn on drapes and hangings.

In this pattern the beads are applied to the design with a diagonal stitch over two close threads of canvas, and the background is filled in with tent stitch using three strands of crewel wool over two close threads of canvas. The lattice pattern is worked in tent stitch in gold thread over two close threads of canvas. (For beading and stitch instructions see page 124.) Each square on the chart represents one bead or one tent stitch of the background.

SIZE 6¾ × 3½in (17 × 9cm)

MATERIALS 18 × 8in (44 × 19cm) double-thread antique canvas, 12 holes to the inch (46 holes/10cm)
Size 9 straw needle for beading
Size 20 tapestry needle
Appleton crewel wool: Royal Blue 825, 1 hank (use three strands)
Cotton sewing thread for applying beads
Madeira gold metallic thread No 8, colour 8013, 1 reel

Mill Hill Glass Seed Beads:

CHRISTMAS GREEN	167	1 pack
WHITE	479	1 pack
YELLOW	128	1 pack
CHRISTMAS RED	165	1 pack

METHOD

1 Find the centre of the canvas by folding in half in both directions and marking the horizontal and vertical lines with a tacking thread.

2 Find the centre of the chart and count on the canvas to the first strawberry to be worked.

3 Thread the straw needle with cotton or similar thread and, using a double thread, apply the beads, working from the first strawberry. Sew all the beaded areas of the design following the coloured beading chart. The beads will lie in the opposite direction to the tent stitch background.

4 Thread the larger tapestry needle with a short length of gold thread, about 14in (36cm) long; a longer length will fray. Work the lattice framework following the chart.

5 Thread the tapestry needle with three strands of crewel wool and work the background in tent stitch to the finish line.

6 To make up the glasses case, see page 121.

Single strawberry motif on the back of the needlecase

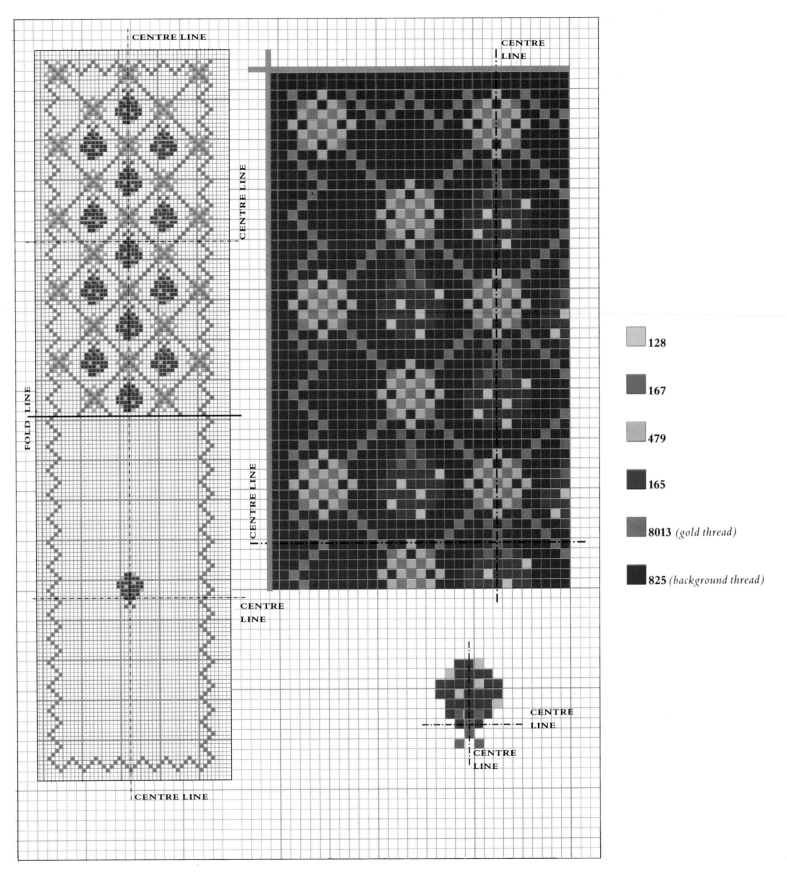

CENTRE LINE

CENTRE
LINE

CENTRE LINE

FOLD LINE

CENTRE LINE

CENTRE
LINE

CENTRE
LINE

CENTRE LINE

128

167

479

165

8013 *(gold thread)*

825 *(background thread)*

BEADED FLOWER BASKET NEEDLECASE

This delightful little needlecase is quick and easy to work, and would make the perfect gift for an enthusiastic needleworker. The beads are applied onto the design with a diagonal stitch over two close threads of canvas. The background is filled in with tent stitch using three strands of crewel wool over two close threads of canvas. (For beading and stitch instructions see page 124.) Each square on the chart represents one bead or one tent stitch of the background.

SIZE 7½ × 4½in (19 × 11cm)

MATERIALS 12 × 9in (30 × 23cm) double-thread antique canvas, 12 holes to the inch (46 holes/10cm)

Size 9 straw needle for beading

Size 20 tapestry needle

Appleton crewel wool: Peacock 647, 1 hank (use three strands)

Cotton sewing thread for applying beads

Mill Hill Glass Seed Beads:

DUSTY ROSE	2005	1 pack
RED	968	1 pack
YELLOW	128	1 pack
ROYAL BLUE	020	1 pack
IRIS	252	1 pack
CHRISTMAS GREEN	167	1 pack
BRONZE	221	1 pack
OLD GOLD	557	1 pack

The delightful Flower Basket Needlecase would make an attractive addition to any workbasket

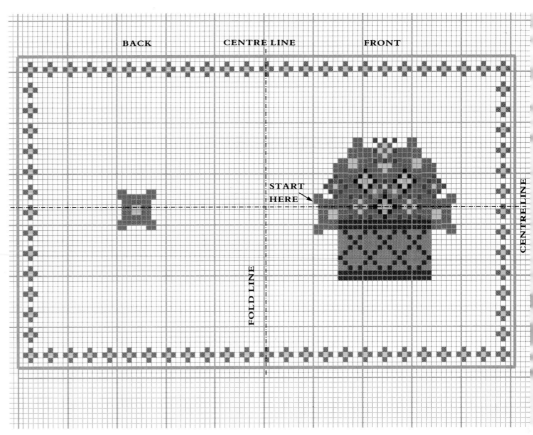

BACK   CENTRE LINE   FRONT

START HERE

FOLD LINE

CENTRE LINE

METHOD

1 Find the centre of the canvas by folding in half in both directions and marking the horizontal and vertical lines with a tacking thread.

2 Find the centre point of the canvas and count to the starting point marked on the chart for the first bead to be worked.

3 Thread the straw needle with cotton or similar thread and, using a double thread, apply the beads, following the coloured beading chart, completing all the beaded parts of the design, the motif on the back and the border. The beads will lie in the opposite direction to the tent stitch background.

4 Thread the larger tapestry needle with three strands of wool and fill in the background in tent stitch.

5 To make up the needlecase see the instructions on page 120.

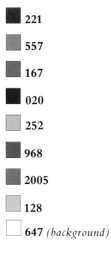

- 221
- 557
- 167
- 020
- 252
- 968
- 2005
- 128
- 647 (*background*)

Chapter Four

Patterns from Around the World

MOST needleworkers today enjoy working on a cushion square. Apart from the pleasure derived from stitching, the end result is a useful decorative item and it makes a small undaunting project which has every possibility of being finished. So all the designs featured in this chapter are for cushion squares.

These designs were inspired by traditional needlework patterns from a number of countries, some geometric and some floral. An intricate floral design using a lot of colour is easier to work in one simple stitch — there is sufficient visual interest in the different colours. On the other hand, a geometric pattern lends itself to the use of a variety of stitches to give an interesting texture to the finished embroidery. Once these fascinating stitches are learnt (all the instructions are given, starting on page 122), they can be used to vary the tent or cross stitch backgrounds

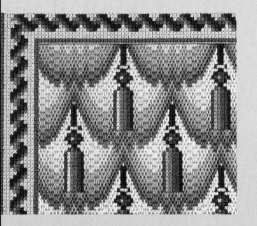

of other designs, which makes for more interesting stitching and gives a more unusual texture. Planning how best to use these stitches can be very absorbing and, because they are often worked over more than one thread of canvas, the work will grow very quickly.

The patterns of the Scottish tartans were much loved by the Victorians and often used in their embroideries. Many of the embroideries were exact replicas of tartans, with skilful interpretation of the complex details of the patterns. The strawberry motif has been used here to complement the tartans.

This design has been worked in two colourways to illustrate the difference between strong vivid colour combinations and soft hazy ones (see page 72). It uses eight textured stitches: tent, brick, cross, chequer, diagonal leaf, Hungarian variation, straight gobelin and slanting gobelin, all of which are worked with three strands of yarn. Because a variety of stitches are used in this design, it is not recommended for complete beginners. (For stitch instructions see

The blue colourway of the Tartan and Strawberries Cushion

pages 122–124.) Each line on the chart represents one thread of canvas.

SIZE 16 × 16in (41 × 41cm)

MATERIALS 20 × 20in (51 × 51cm) mono de luxe antique or white (for paler colourway) canvas, 14 holes to the inch (56 holes/10cm) Size 20 tapestry needle
Appleton crewel wool (use three strands):

RED COLOURWAY

SCARLET	504	1¼ hanks
ROSE PINK	758	¼ hank
CORAL	863	¼ hank
BROWN OLIVE	312	2¼ hanks
GRASS GREEN	254	¾ hank
PURPLE	106	½ hank
WHITE	992	¾ hank

BLUE COLOURWAY (in brackets on chart key)

BRIGHT CHINA BLUE	743	1¼ hanks
BRIGHT CHINA BLUE	746	¼ hank
BRIGHT CHINA BLUE	741	¼ hank
CHOCOLATE	181	2¼ hanks
CHOCOLATE	182	¾ hank
ELEPHANT	976	½ hank
WHITE	992	¾ hank

METHOD

1 Find the centre of the canvas by folding in half in both directions and marking the horizontal and vertical lines with a tacking thread.
2 Following the colour code, start from the centre using three strands of yarn for each stitch.
3 Work cross stitch and diagonal leaf stitch pattern in centre and strawberries in chequer stitch.
4 Fill in the background with tent stitch and complete with a row of cross stitch and slanting gobelin.
5 Continue to work each border pattern from the centre line, following the colour code and counting the stitches onto the canvas, referring to the stitch instructions. Complete each one before starting the next.
6 To make up the cushion, see the instructions on page 119.

START
HERE

NTRE
LINE

CENTRE
LINE

	504 (743)		863 (741)		254 (182)		992 (992)
	758 (746)		312 (181)		106 (976)		312 (181) *(background)*

ENGLISH FLOWER GARDEN CUSHION

Inspired by a tapestry design from the early part of this century, this pattern is cleverly arranged so that the flowers repeat both diagonally and horizontally across the canvas. Any shape or size could be worked, from a small footstool to a large chair cover. It could also be made into a rug, finished off with a simple border repeating the colours in the flowers of the central pattern.

Although this design is worked on a 12 holes to the inch (46 holes/10cm) mesh canvas, other counts could be used, from a fine small mesh which would give a smaller more delicate result, to a large rug canvas (with different quantities of yarn). This interesting pattern gives plenty of scope for experimenting with colour as well as size. A paler shade of background yarn would give a softer delicate look, or a clearer, stronger background colour would give a more vivid and dramatic image.

This design uses only tent stitch for the main design area, but gobelin stitch could be used for the border pattern (see pages 123–124 for stitch instructions). Each square on the chart represents one stitch.

SIZE 16½ × 16½in (42 × 42cm)

MATERIALS 21 × 21in (53 × 53cm) white mono de luxe canvas, 12 holes to the inch (46 holes/10cm), or 4in (10cm) larger than the finished design
Size 18 tapestry needle
Appleton tapestry wool (use one strand):

PASTEL MAUVE	884	1 skein
PURPLE	101	1 skein
PURPLE	104	1 skein
CORNFLOWER	461	1 skein
CORNFLOWER	462	1 skein
CORNFLOWER	463	1 skein
CORNFLOWER	464	1 skein
BRIGHT PEACOCK	831	1 skein
BRIGHT PEACOCK	832	¼ hank
BRIGHT PEACOCK	833	1 skein
LEMON	996	1 skein
AUTUMN YELLOW	472	1 skein

OPPOSITE The English Flower Garden Cushion uses a palette of many colours to achieve its country-garden atmosphere

78

(continued overleaf)

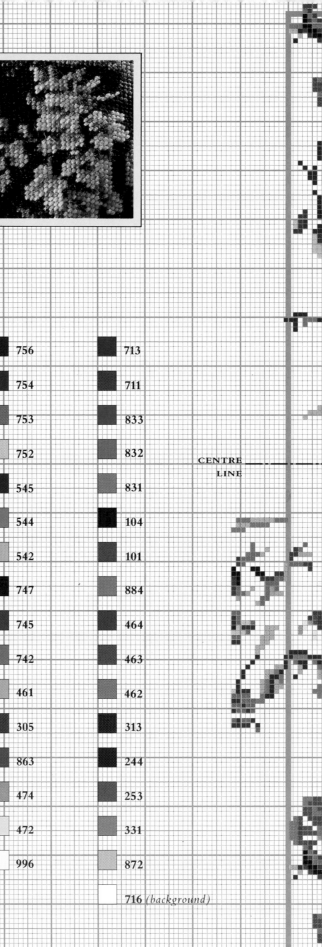

AUTUMN YELLOW	474	¼ hank
CORAL	863	1 skein
RED FAWN	305	1 skein
EARLY ENGLISH GREEN	542	¼ hank
EARLY ENGLISH GREEN	544	½ hank
EARLY ENGLISH GREEN	545	½ hank
BRIGHT CHINA BLUE	742	1 skein
BRIGHT CHINA BLUE	745	1 skein
BRIGHT CHINA BLUE	747	1 skein
ROSE PINK	752	¼ hank
ROSE PINK	753	1 skein
ROSE PINK	754	1 skein
ROSE PINK	756	1 skein
BROWN OLIVE	313	1 skein
PASTEL YELLOW	872	1 hank
DRAB GREEN	331	1 skein
GRASS GREEN	253	1 skein
OLIVE GREEN	244	1 skein
WINE RED	711	1 skein
WINE RED	713	1 skein
BACKGROUND		
WINE RED	716	4 hanks

METHOD

1 Find the centre of the canvas by folding it in half in both directions and marking the horizontal and vertical lines with a tacking thread.

2 Using one strand of tapestry wool, start from the centre and work the first motif in tent stitch, following the chart and the colour code. Continue working the pattern and filling in the background as work progresses to the edge of the border.

3 Work the border in gobelin stitch over two threads of canvas.

4 To make up the cushion see the instructions on page 119.

■ 756		■ 713	
■ 754		■ 711	
■ 753		■ 833	
■ 752		■ 832	
■ 545		■ 831	
■ 544		■ 104	
■ 542		■ 101	
■ 747		■ 884	
■ 745		■ 464	
■ 742		■ 463	
■ 461		■ 462	
■ 305		■ 313	
■ 863		■ 244	
■ 474		■ 253	
■ 472		■ 331	
□ 996		■ 872	
		□ 716 *(background)*	

CENTRE LINE

CENTRE LINE

CENTRE LINE

$\mathscr{B}$OKHARA $\mathscr{C}$USHION

Rich and colourful embroideries from Turkey, Greece and Persia give an insight into the way of life of the eastern Mediterranean. In the fine collection belonging to The Embroiderers' Guild at Hampton Court Palace in south-west London are many such pieces, one of which inspired this design.

The design uses four decorative stitches: tent, cross, straight gobelin and slanting gobelin. Because of the number of different stitches used, this design is not recommended for a complete beginner. (For stitch instructions see pages 122–124.) Each line on the chart represents one thread of canvas.

SIZE 16 × 15½in (41 × 39cm)

MATERIALS 19½ × 19½in (50 × 50cm) mono de luxe antique canvas, 14 holes to the inch (56 holes/10cm)
Size 20 tapestry needle

Appleton crewel wool (use three strands):

BRIGHT TERRACOTTA	224	1 hank
BRIGHT TERRACOTTA	226	½ hank
BROWN GROUNDING	586	1 skein
BROWN OLIVE	311	½ hank
BRIGHT PEACOCK	833	½ hank
GRASS GREEN	254	½ hank
BRIGHT CHINA BLUE	747	2½ hanks

METHOD

1 Find the centre of the canvas by folding in half in both directions and marking the horizontal and vertical lines with a tacking thread.
2 Use three strands of yarn throughout. Count from the chart and use colours according to colour key to work the stitches from the instructions on pages 122–124.
3 Counting the threads of canvas from the centre, work the inner border of cross stitches.
4 Work each diagonal band starting from the corner of the cross-stitch inner border and fill in the background of each part with tent stitch. To finish, complete the border.
5 To make up the cushion, see page 119.

OPPOSITE The lively combination of pattern and colour in the Bokhara Cushion produces a warm Mediterranean feel, and the textured stitches give an interesting finish

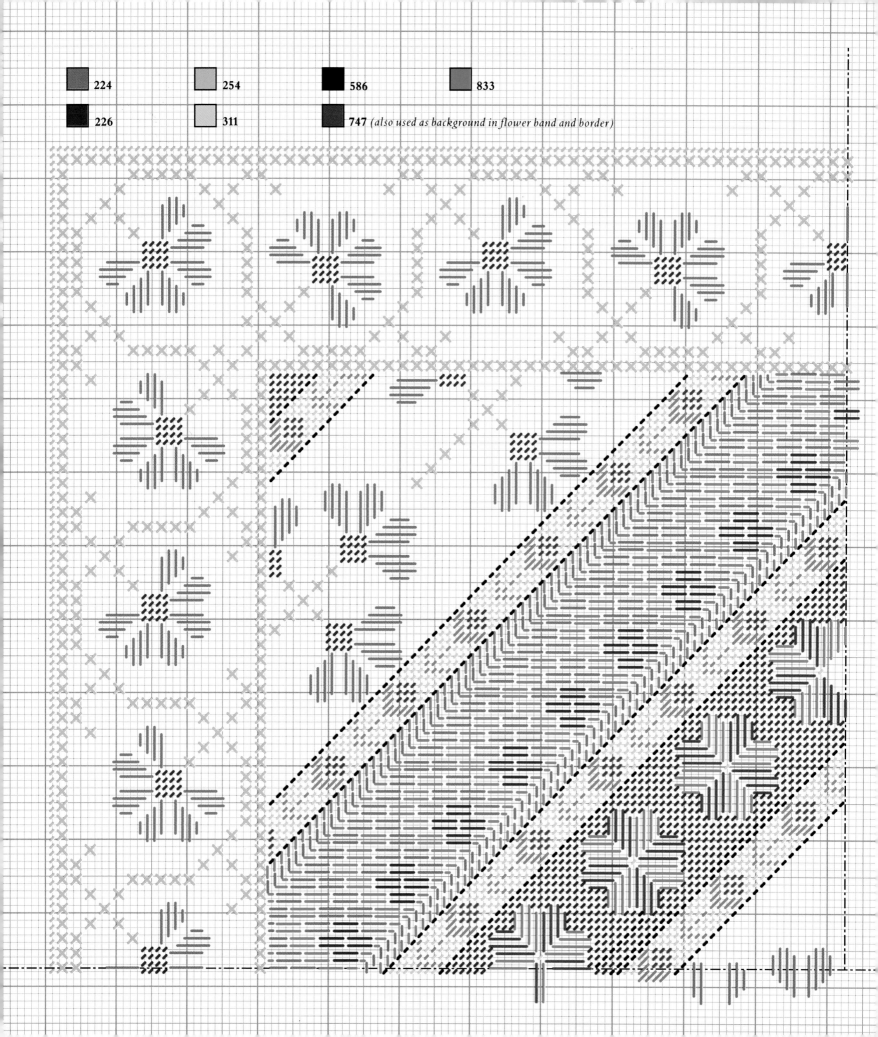

224 254 586 833
226 311 747 *(also used as background in flower band and border)*

CENTRE LINE

CENTRE LINE

START HERE

Florentine Tassels Cushion

The popular Florentine pattern used in this design is easy and quick to work, as the stitches are sewn over more than one thread of the canvas at a time. The tassel motif (popular with the Victorians for borders) is used throughout the design to create a more interesting project to work, and to prevent the Florentine embroidery from becoming repetitive. The whole design is finished off with a twisting rope border to match the tassels.

Although the design is shown here in a pale-green background with stronger colours for the tassels, another pastel background with toning colours would be just as effective, and a grey background with white and black tassels would look stunning.

This design uses three decorative textured stitches, Florentine, cross and tent stitch, and all the stitches use three strands of yarn. Because the cushion is quick and easy to make, it is well suited for a beginner. (For stitch instructions see pages 122–124.) Each line on the chart represents one thread of canvas.

SIZE 13 × 14in (33 × 36cm)

MATERIALS 19 × 19in (48 × 48cm) mono de luxe antique canvas, 14 holes to the inch (56 holes/10cm)
Size 20 tapestry needle

Appleton crewel wool (use three strands):

FLORENTINE BACKGROUND COLOURS

GREY GREEN	355★	½ hank
GREY GREEN	354	¼ hank
GREY GREEN	353★	½ hank
GREY GREEN	352	½ hank
PASTEL	874†	1¼ hanks
PASTEL	873	½ hank

BLUE TASSELS

DULL MARINE BLUE	325★	¼ hank
DULL MARINE BLUE	324★	¼ hank
DULL MARINE BLUE	322	1 skein
DULL MARINE BLUE	321★	¼ hank
PASTEL	875	1 skein

OPPOSITE The Florentine Tassels Cushion design sets a traditional Victorian tassel pattern against a subtle background of Florentine stitch

PINK TASSELS

BRIGHT TERRACOTTA	226★	¼ hank
BRIGHT TERRACOTTA	224★	¼ hank
BRIGHT TERRACOTTA	223	1 skein
BRIGHT TERRACOTTA	222★	¼ hank
BRIGHT TERRACOTTA	221	1 skein

★ colours also used in rope border pattern

† border background colour (see page 86)

METHOD

1 Find the centre of the canvas by folding in half in both directions and marking the horizontal and vertical lines with a tacking thread.

2 Using three strands of yarn throughout, start from the centre with the first cross stitch.

3 Complete the first tassel and continue by fil-ling in the background around the first motif in Florentine stitch.

4 Work the Florentine pattern to the next tassel motif and continue counting and working the motifs and the background from the chart until the centre pattern is completed.

5 Work one row of tent and then one row of cross stitch around the central design before commencing the outer border. Counting from the first row of cross stitch, start the rope border from the centre line in cross stitch and complete the background by filling in with cross stitch.

6 Finish with a row of cross stitch and then a row of tent stitch.

7 To make up the cushion, see instructions on page 119.

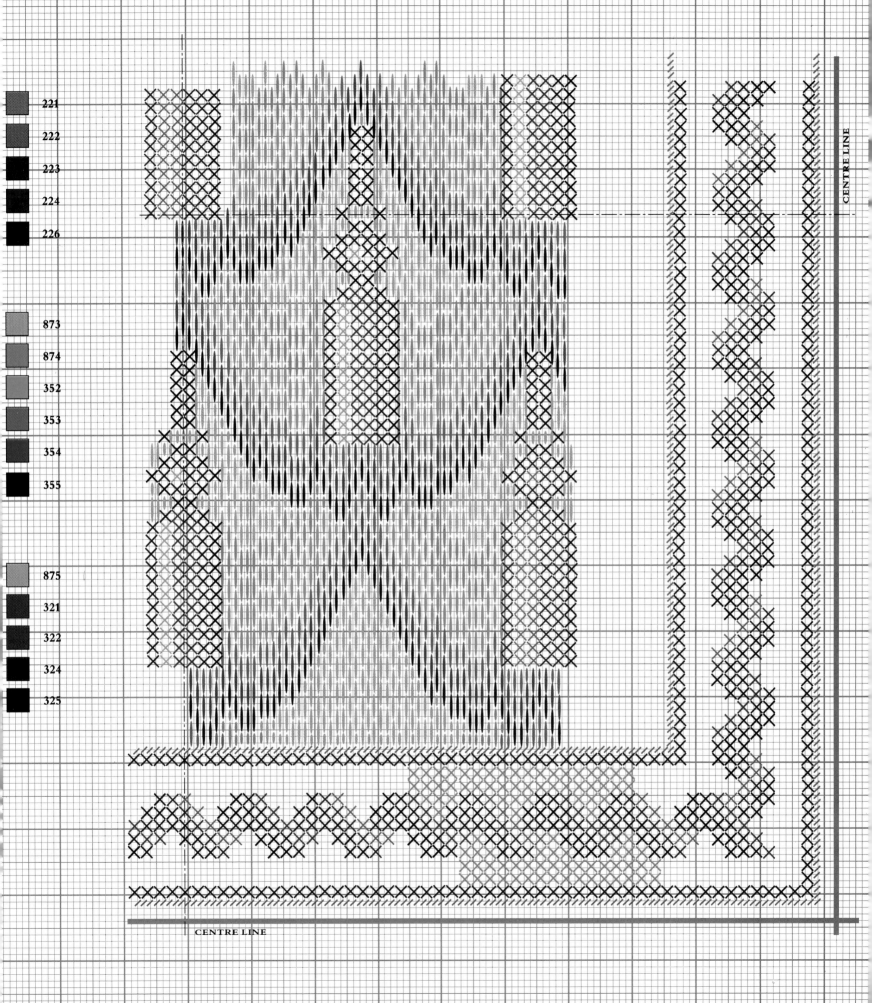

221

222

223

224

226

873

874

352

353

354

355

875

321

322

324

325

CENTRE LINE

CENTRE LINE

Chapter Five

BORDER PATTERNS

*T*HERE is no doubt that a piece of canvas work is improved by the addition of a border, which will not only frame and balance the work, but also gives the design an individual touch. It is probably worth experimenting with different colours and border patterns on a spare piece of canvas before deciding on which to use. Scale can be very important, as some patterns can take a wide border and others are better with a simple narrow one. Many borders are worked in tent stitch and reflect the pattern or motif used in the central design; others are worked in a

combination of different stitches and repeated sequences.

There are differing degrees of complexity when it comes to borders. The easiest are undoubtedly those using straight stitches, like the gobelin border used on Queen Mary's Tree Cushion (page 14). A more interesting effect is easily achieved by using two colours, working one row in one colour and the next in another. There is no need to count these borders onto the finished design as they will always fit.

Borders using wider stitches worked over two or more threads of the canvas are probably a little more difficult. With these, the number of threads along each side of the worked area of the design must be counted, to see whether the chosen stitch combination will fit round the design to meet in the corners. Sometimes extra rows must be worked to the main pattern so that the border will fit.

A simple way of creating a border, which would not entail any counting, would be to tack a diagonal line from the centre of the design to the corner of the planned finish line. The stitches could then just be worked up to this diagonal line and started again along the next edge of the design, leaving a neat mitred effect.

The most difficult borders to achieve are the repeating intertwined borders, which are traditionally used on samplers. On these, the mitred corners need to fall in exactly the right place to contain the central design, so the pattern will have to be drawn onto graph paper first, counting each line of the graph paper as a thread of canvas and positioning the centre of the border to fit the centre of the finished edge of the design.

There are two ingenious ways of working out mitred corners. One uses a small handbag mirror. When the design has been worked onto the graph paper, place the small mirror diagonally across the border at the most suitable place for turning so that the design is reflected at right angles, and use the mirror image as a guide for working the next part of the pattern. Alternatively, make a tracing from the wrong side of the original and put the two together at right-angles at the correct point. Then make a final tracing of the mitre, which can be counted and drawn onto the graph.

The border patterns featured in this chapter have been divided into three groups: simple borders worked in yellows and blues; slightly more complicated borders, worked in corals and greens; then, the more difficult intertwining patterns, worked in greens and pinks. Finally, there are two pretty flower borders worked in tent stitch. Both are simple to work, but they need to be counted onto the canvas to ensure the mitred corners fit. They would be useful patterns to mix with others to create the sort of design used for the cover of the gentleman's gout stool (page 110). They would also make attractive border patterns for a cushion cover. Finally, A Pot-pourri of Patterns brings

together a variety of patterns and stitches from this book to make a fascinating new cushion design.

I hope this small collection of border designs will encourage you to experiment and even design and work your own combinations of different stitches, bringing a really personal touch to your canvas embroidery.

One strand of tapestry wool has been used to work all the borders. For each border follow the chart, counting the stitches onto the canvas. For stitch instructions see pages 122–124.

Yellow and Blue Borders

These easy borders use straight gobelin or cushion stitch. Patterns six and ten (see overleaf) do not need counting and can be worked straight onto the canvas. All the rest have mitred corners. To do this, draw a line from the corner of the central design to the corner edge of the area of canvas to be worked, then work the pattern as far as this diagonal line. Restart and reverse the pattern to match the first side. (For stitch instructions see pages 122 and 123.) Each line on the chart represents one thread of canvas.

PATTERN ONE Use four colours, stitch in straight gobelin over a varying number of threads of canvas.

PATTERN TWO Use three colours, stitch in straight gobelin over a varying number of threads of canvas.

PATTERN THREE Use three colours, stitch in straight gobelin over four threads of canvas throughout.

PATTERN FOUR Use four colours, stitch in straight gobelin over a varying number of threads of canvas.

PATTERN FIVE Use two colours, stitch in straight gobelin over a varying number of threads of canvas.

PATTERN SIX Use two colours, stitch in straight gobelin over two threads of canvas throughout.

PATTERN SEVEN Use two colours, stitch in straight gobelin over a varying number of threads of canvas.

PATTERN EIGHT Use six colours, stitch in cushion stitch.

PATTERN NINE Use two colours, stitch in straight gobelin over a varying number of threads of canvas.

PATTERN TEN Use two colours, stitch in straight gobelin and cushion stitch.

OPPOSITE *These very simple borders use straight gobelin or cushion stitch*

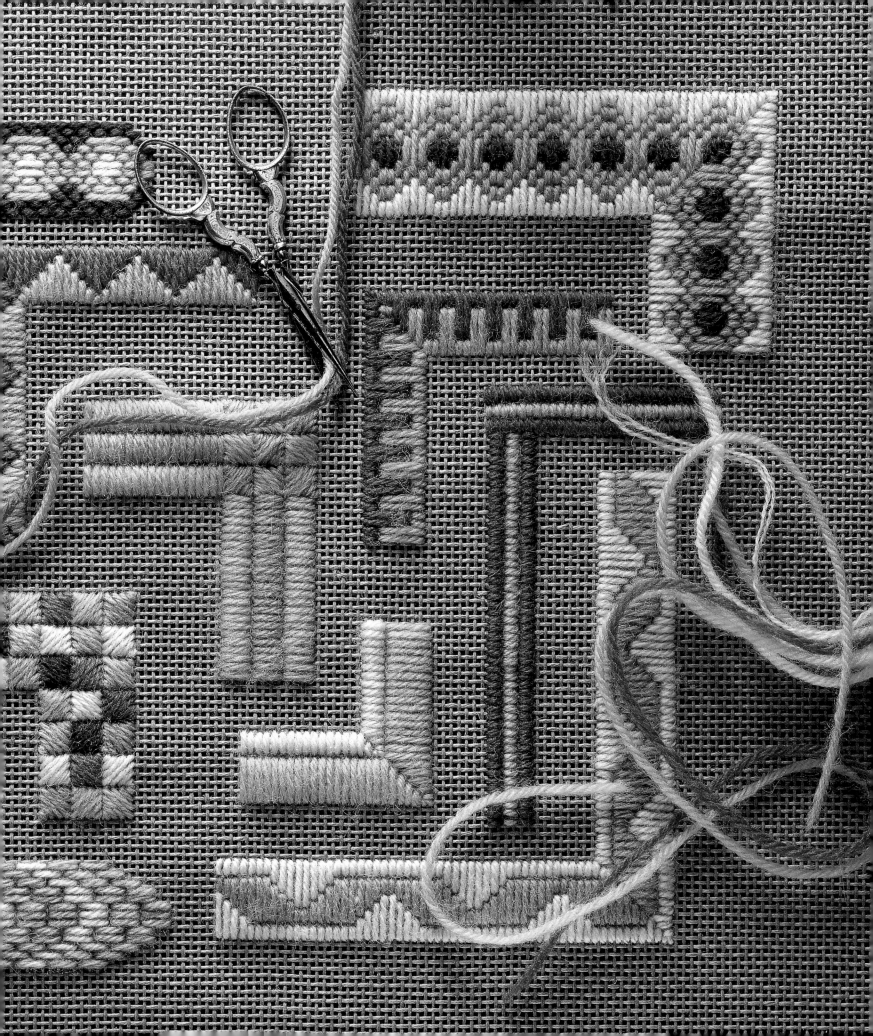

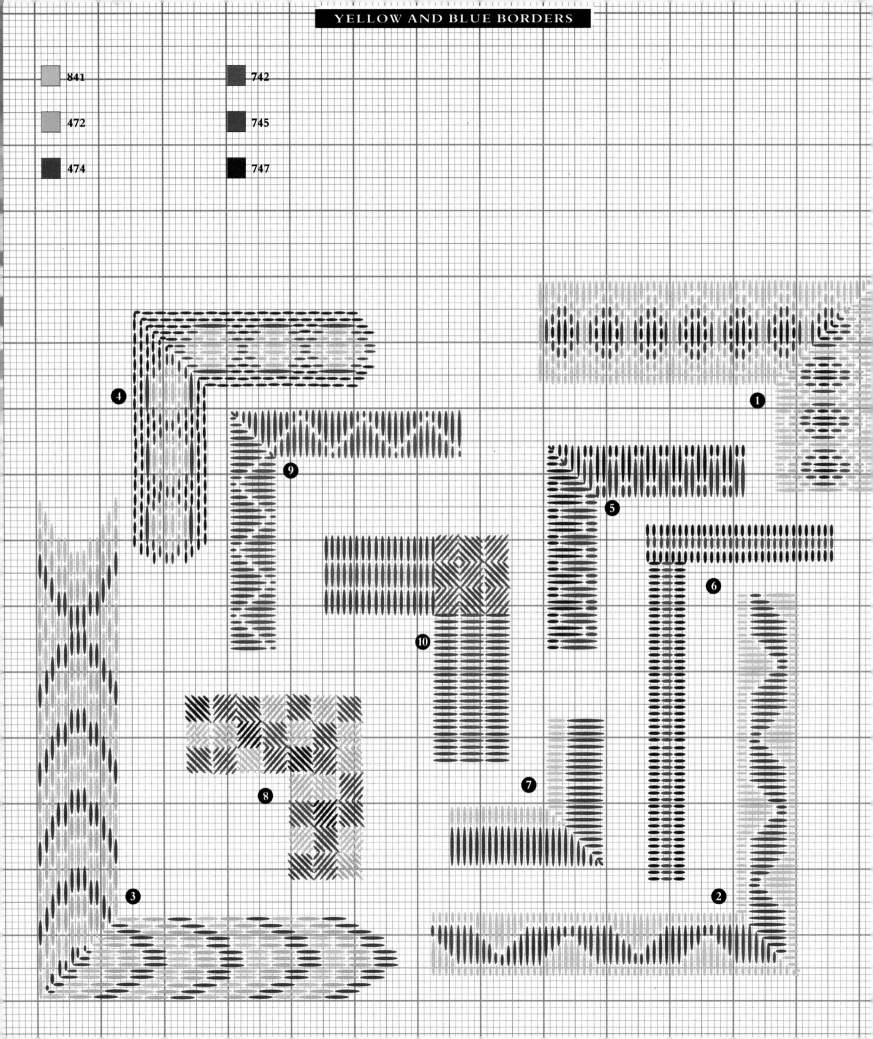

CORAL AND GREEN BORDERS

881   251   255   861   863   726

CORAL AND GREEN BORDERS

The patterns for these borders are generally fairly easy to work. The stitches used are mostly straight, and because they are worked over a varying number of threads of canvas, there is an interesting selection of borders to choose from. These designs will need to be counted and centred onto the canvas at the right place so that the mitred corners fall at the correct position of the repeat. (For stitch instructions see pages 122–123.) Each line on the chart represents one thread of canvas.

PATTERN ONE Use two colours, stitch in straight gobelin over a varying number of threads of canvas.

PATTERN TWO Use three colours, stitch in straight gobelin over a varying number of threads of canvas.

PATTERN THREE Use three colours, stitch in straight gobelin over a varying number of threads of canvas.

PATTERN FOUR Use two colours, stitch in cushion stitch.

PATTERN FIVE Use three colours, stitch in straight gobelin over a varying number of threads of canvas.

PATTERN SIX Use three colours, stitch in straight gobelin over a varying number of threads of canvas.

PATTERN SEVEN Use two colours, stitch in straight gobelin over a varying number of threads of canvas.

These fairly easy borders use mostly straight stitches

$\mathcal{P}$INK AND $\mathcal{G}$REEN $\mathcal{B}$ORDERS

These floral patterns are useful for finishing off a sampler. They are a little more difficult to work, but as they are repeating patterns they become easier as work progresses. All these borders need to be worked out on graph paper to centre them on the canvas and position the mitred corners. The mitres do not have to be identical to those shown here. (See page 123 for guidance on mitring corners.) The backgrounds should be finished in tent stitch (not shown here. For stitch instructions see pages 122–124.) Each line on the chart represents one thread of canvas.

PATTERN ONE Use four colours. First, work a portion of the curving cross stitches, then the flowers in straight gobelin before filling in the centres of the flowers with single cross stitches. Work the tent-stitch background as the pattern progresses.

PATTERN TWO Use four colours. First, work the straight gobelin stitches, leaving spaces for the cross stitches to twine in and out of the line. Then work the cross stitches and, lastly, fill in with the arrowhead stitch. Fill in the tent-stitch background as the pattern progresses. Work each section of border before moving on to the next.

PATTERN THREE Use three colours. First, work a portion of the curving cross stitch, then the leaf and sloping gobelin stitches. Next, work the strawberries in brick stitch and fill in the background with tent stitch.

PATTERN FOUR Use three colours. First, work a length of the curving cross stitch. Then work the cross stitch beneath the flowers. Fill in each section with a flower in cushion stitch. Fill in the tent-stitch background as the pattern progresses.

PATTERN FIVE Use four colours. First, work a portion of the curving tent stitch. Then work the diagonal leaf stitch. Fill in the tent-stitch background as the pattern progresses.

These more intricate floral borders use textured stitches in repeating patterns

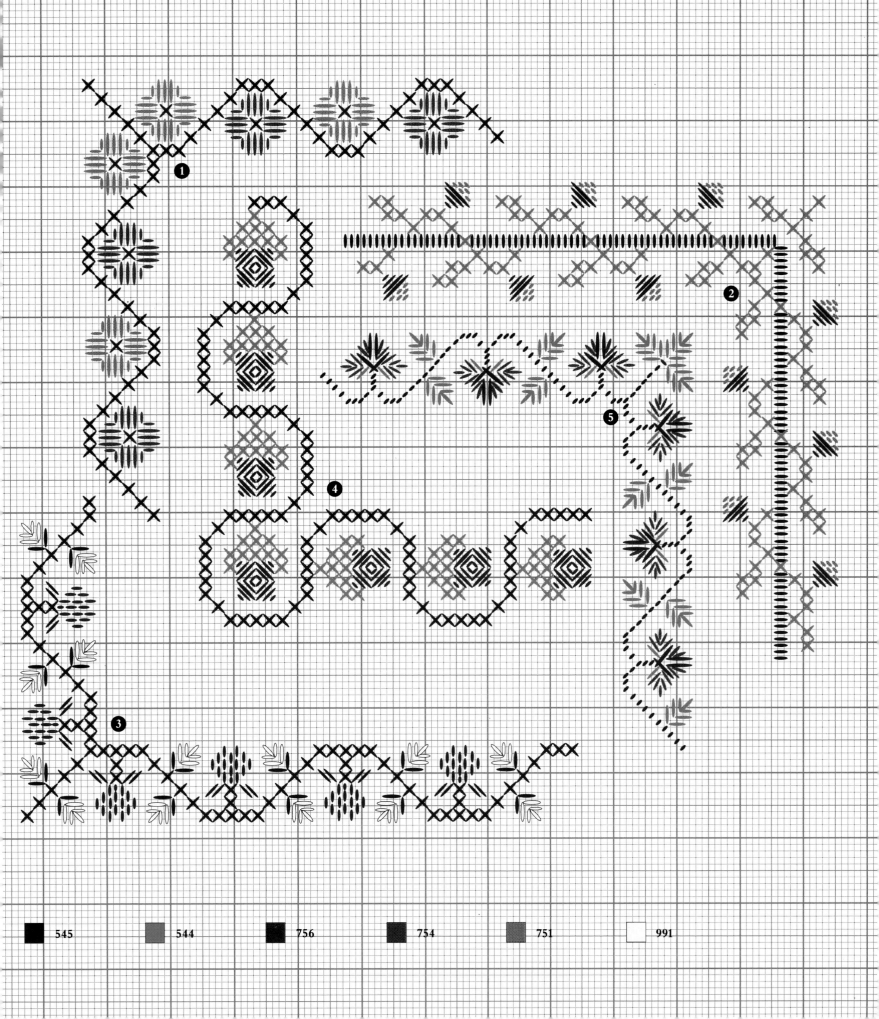

545   544   756   754   751   991

Rose Border

This border of pink rosebuds and roses set amongst leaves creates a traditional pattern for a cushion square or sampler. The pattern has been reversed in the middle of each section so that the corners link up well. This border could be extended by repeating the pattern or, alternatively, it could be reduced by omitting a small section. This pattern, which is worked in tent stitch, could also be worked in bands across the canvas for a cushion cover or square footstool, or one band could be worked to make a bell pull. (For stitch instructions see page 124.) Each square on the chart represents one stitch on the canvas.

SIZE 19 × 18in (48 × 46cm)

MATERIALS Mono de luxe antique canvas, 12 holes to the inch (46 holes/10cm)
Size 18 tapestry needle
Appleton tapestry wool (use one strand):

ROSE PINK	751	½ hank
ROSE PINK	754	½ hank
ROSE PINK	755	½ hank
BRIGHT YELLOW	551	¼ hank
EARLY ENGLISH GREEN	543	½ hank
EARLY ENGLISH GREEN	545	½ hank

METHOD

1 Following the colour code and counting the stitches from the chart onto the canvas, working in tent stitch, start from the centre line, filling in the background as work progresses.

The pretty Rose Border would make an ideal traditional 'frame' for a cushion or sampler

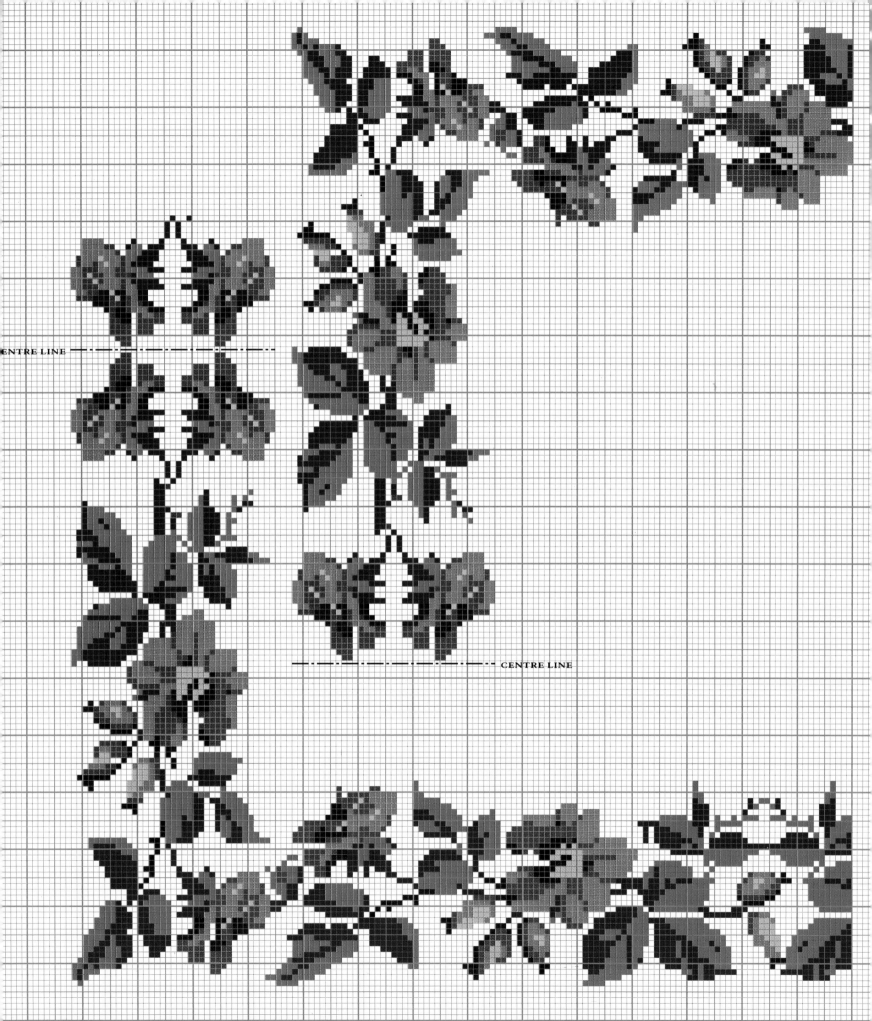

CENTRE LINE

CENTRE LINE

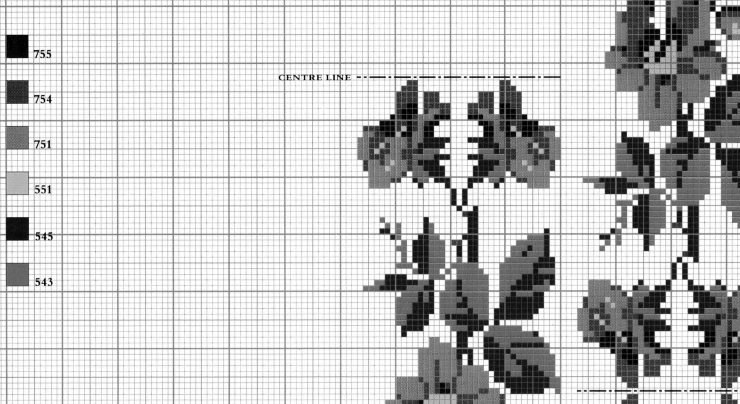

755

754

751

551

545

543

CENTRE LINE --- --- --- --- --- --- --- ---

CENTRE LINE

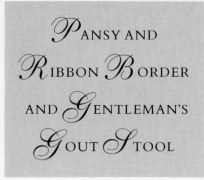

Pansy and Ribbon Border and Gentleman's Gout Stool

The delicate colouring used to work this border has produced a soft attractive design of cornflowers, pansies and leaves tied with a ribbon. It has been made to form a frame with the pattern reversed in the centre at the top and bottom so that the bows work correctly at each corner. The photograph on page 110 shows this design worked in bands, with a barley-twist pattern between each band, and then used to cover a gentleman's gout stool – a good example of how border patterns can be developed into complete projects. This pattern can be extended lengthwise and widthwise to fit any shape (for example, a bell pull).

Other colour combinations could be used to produce a much stronger pattern. The design is worked in tent stitch. (For stitch instructions see page 124.) Each square on the chart represents one stitch on the canvas.

PATTERN REPEAT Every 60 threads

MATERIALS Mono de luxe antique canvas, 12 holes to the inch (46 holes/10cm)
Size 18 tapestry needle
Appleton tapestry wool (use one strand).
The following quantities are for one pattern repeat:

HERALDIC GOLD	841	½ hank
HERALDIC GOLD	842	¼ hank
HERALDIC GOLD	843	¼ hank
PURPLE	102	1 skein
PURPLE	103	1 skein
BRIGHT CHINA BLUE	742	1 skein
BRIGHT CHINA BLUE	746	1 skein
EARLY ENGLISH GREEN	543	1 skein
EARLY ENGLISH GREEN	546	1 skein
BACKGROUND		
BROWN GROUNDING	588	1 hank

METHOD

1 Following the colour code and counting the stitches from the chart onto the canvas, working in tent stitch, start from the centre line, filling in the background as work progresses.

OPPOSITE The Pansy and Ribbon Border is a repeating pattern which makes an ideal border and can also be used across the canvas as seen on the Gentleman's Gout Stool (page 110)

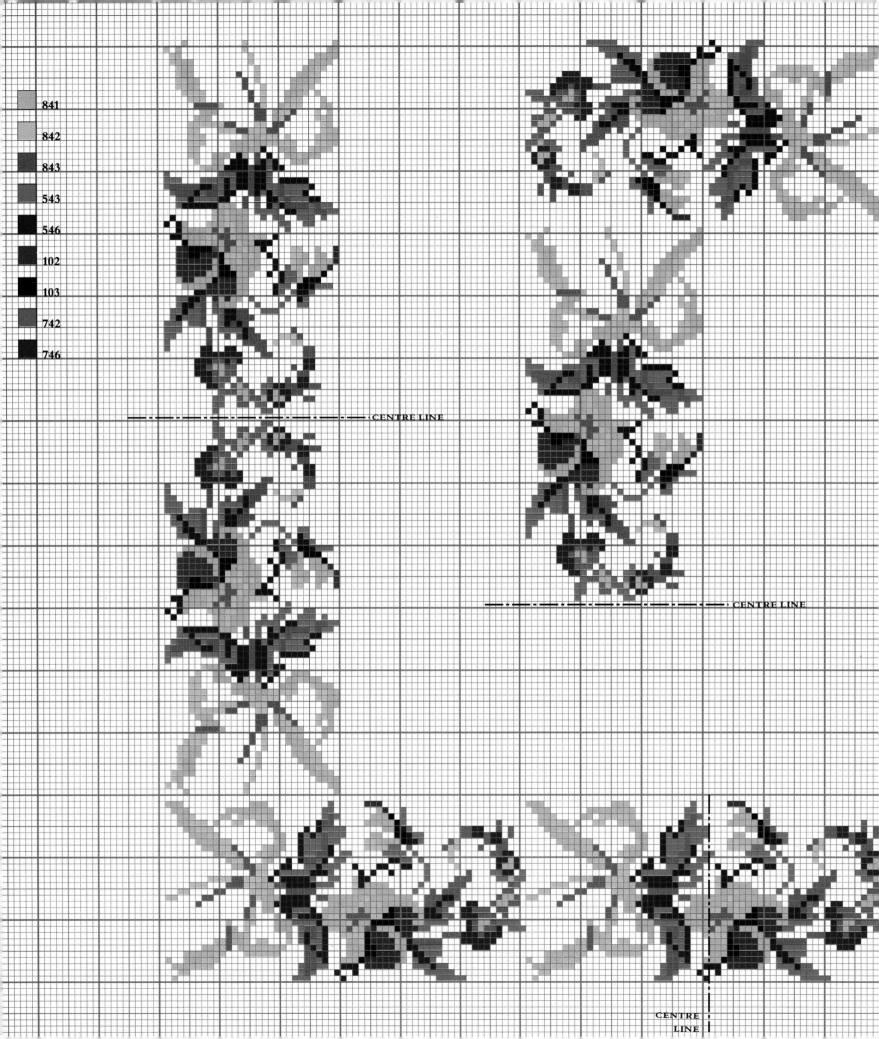

841

842

843

543

546

102

103

742

746

CENTRE LINE

CENTRE LINE

CENTRE
LINE

CENTRE
LINE

CENTRE LINE

CENTRE LINE

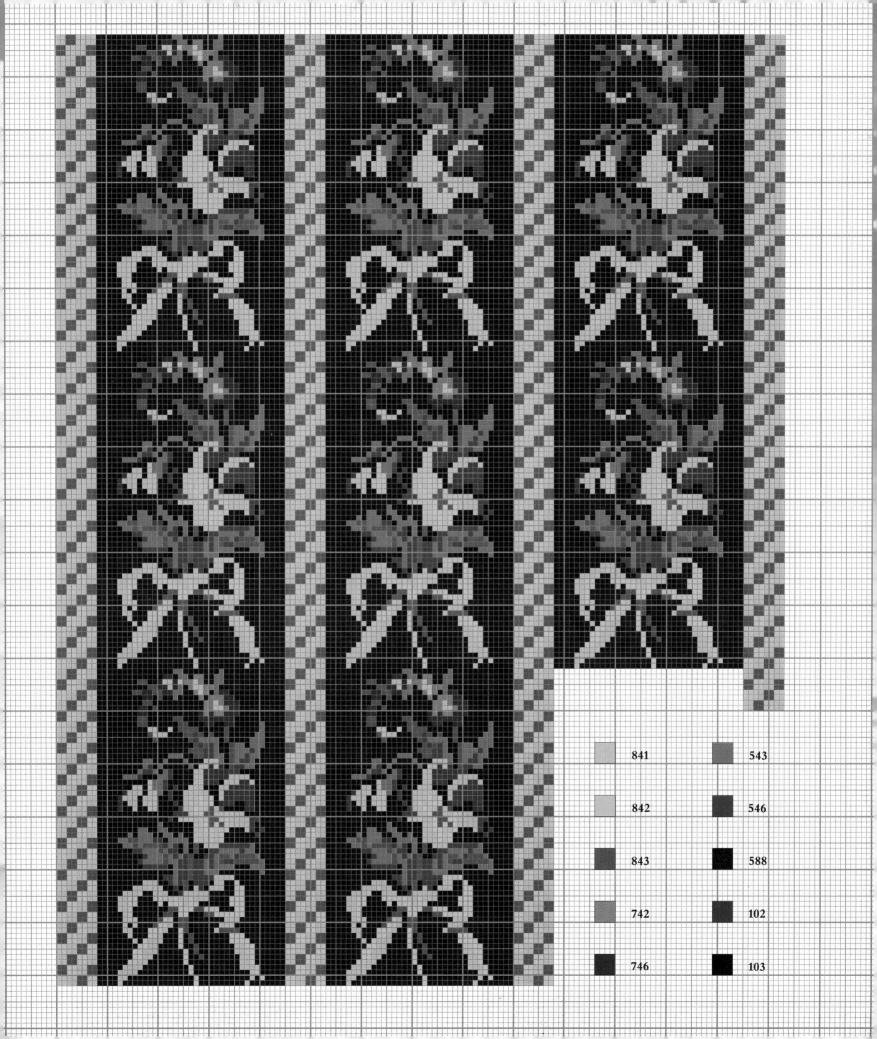

	841		543
	842		546
	843		588
	742		102
	746		103

A Pot-pourri Of Patterns

This design brings together a variety of stitches and patterns that have been used throughout this book, and illustrates how they can be used together to create a complete design using only six shades of pink, green and white. By restricting the use of colours, what may look like a difficult design is made relatively simple, and I hope it will give you encouragement and inspiration to experiment with other patterns and stitches in this book – so that you will be able to produce your own very personal piece of work. Each line on the chart represents one thread of canvas.

SIZE 13¾ × 14¼in (35 × 36cm)

MATERIALS 20 × 20in (50 × 50cm) mono de luxe antique canvas, 12 holes to the inch (46 holes/10cm)
Size 18 tapestry needle

Appleton tapestry wool (use one strand):

WHITE	992	½ hank
ROSE PINK	751	1 hank
ROSE PINK	753	½ hank
BRIGHT TERRACOTTA	222	1 hank
EARLY ENGLISH GREEN	542	1 hank
EARLY ENGLISH GREEN	545	1½ hanks

METHOD

1 Find the centre of the canvas by folding in half in both directions and marking the horizontal and vertical lines with a tacking thread.
2 Following the colour code, and using one strand of yarn, begin at the centre and work the first stitch of the cushion pattern.
3 Complete each pattern before starting on the next. Refer to the stitch directory (pages 122–124) and count the stitches from the chart onto the canvas.

The Pot-pourri Cushion has been created by combining different patterns from elsewhere in this book

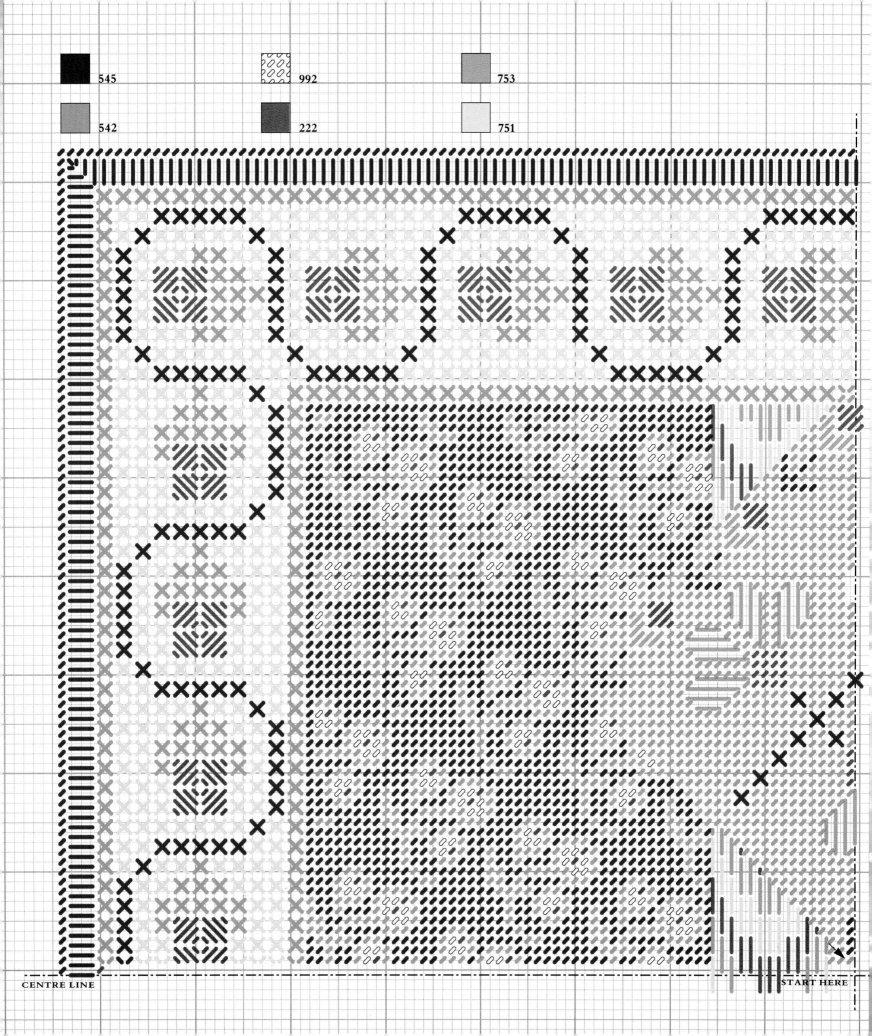

545

992

753

542

222

751

CENTRE LINE

START HERE

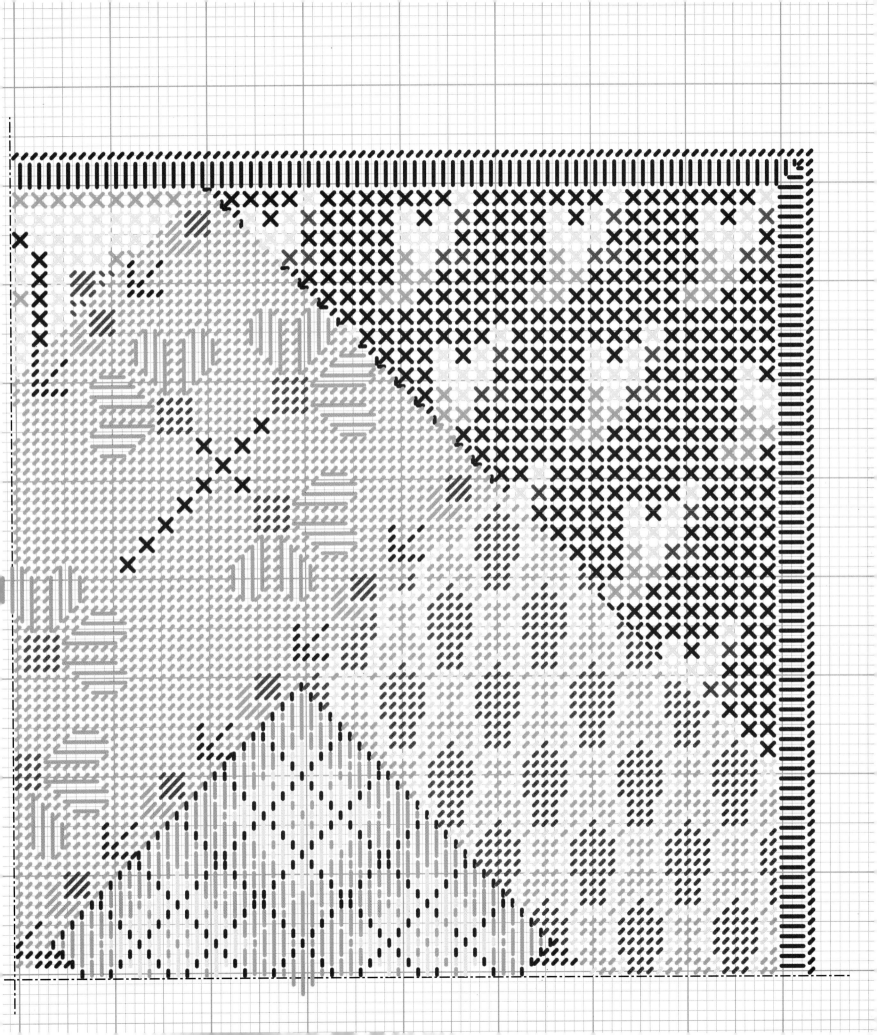

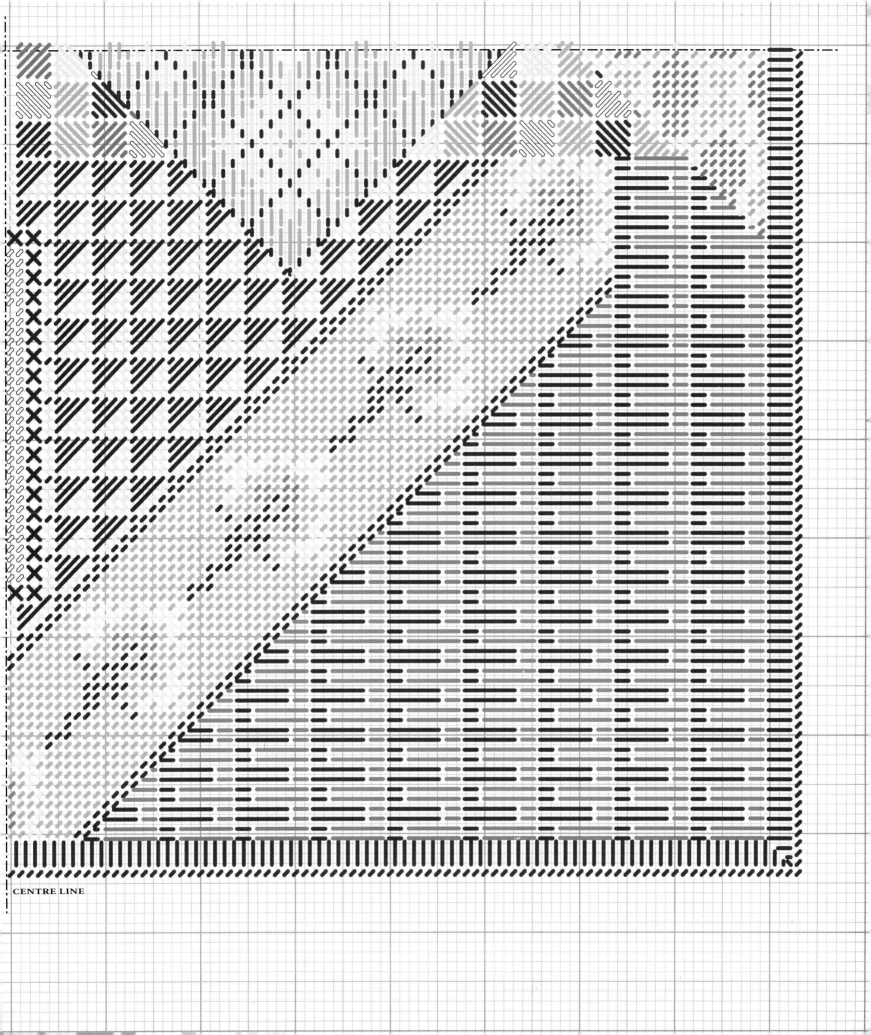

CENTRE LINE

FINISHING AND MAKING UP TECHNIQUES

*A*LMOST *all stitched canvases are distorted because the process of stitching, particularly when using diagonal stitches, pulls the canvas out of shape. This can be minimised by using a roller frame during stitching, but most canvases will still need stretching (blocking) to achieve a straight and pleasing finished result, even if they are not going to be made into framed pictures.*

Some canvases may be quite difficult to stretch, so I would advise using a professional stretching and framing service – this should prevent disappointment after your many hours of work. Often, your local needlecraft retailer will be able to recommend or even offer such a service. A similar case could also be made for using a professional to make up the final projects, such as cushions and seat covers. However, if you wish to tackle your own stretching, framing and making-up, I hope the following instructions will be useful.

Stretching

MATERIALS

- Wooden board larger than the canvas and soft enough to take tacks or nails
- Small tacks or stainless steel nails
- Piece of blotting paper larger than the finished design (or use two pieces joined together)
- Set square and ruler
- Hammer and pliers
- Pencil or waterproof marker

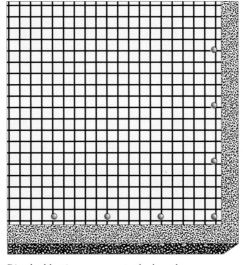

Pin the blotting paper onto the board

To prepare the board for stretching, draw grid lines onto the blotting paper at 1in (2.5cm) intervals horizontally and vertically and pin it to the board. Moisten the back of the canvas with a fairly wet (but not dripping) sponge and place canvas face up over the squared blotting paper, using the drawn lines on the blotting paper as a guide to get the sides straight and the corners square. Tack it in place, gently pulling back into shape and placing the tacks 1in (2.5cm) from the edge of the design and 1in (2.5cm) apart. Do not hammer the tacks right into the board because, as the canvas is pulled and stretched, the tacks may have to be removed and repositioned. When the

Tack the canvas onto the blotting paper

canvas is completely square, knock the tacks firmly into the board, possibly adding more tacks at ½in (12mm) to ¼in (6mm) intervals so that the canvas is completely taut, but never stretch the canvas so tightly that the threads are straining against the tacks. Leave it to dry naturally in a horizontal position away from direct heat or sunshine for as long as possible (36 to 48 hours). Badly distorted canvases might need stretching more than once.

If a template has been used, draw the template outline on to the blotting paper and then follow the instructions above to stretch the canvas so that it fits the template perfectly. If the design is worked entirely in tent stitch, stretch the canvas face down on the blotting paper to even out the surface of the stitched canvas. If textured stitches have been used, stretch right side up so that the stitches are not flattened. Beaded designs should also be stretched right side up.

Framing

It is advisable to use a good professional framer, but if this is not possible, here are a few guidelines.

MATERIALS

■ Piece of hardboard to fit into the recess of your chosen frame, which can be slightly larger than the worked area to give a margin of unworked canvas
■ Strong cotton thread to lace across the board
■ Tacks
■ Large tapestry needle
■ Small hammer

1 Stretch the canvas back into shape if necessary, following the instructions on page 118.
2 Place the canvas face down on a clean surface and centre the board on the back of the canvas.
3 Thread the tapestry needle with strong cotton thread and lace the canvas onto the board from top to bottom and from side to side, pulling and holding the thread to make sure the design stays centred and straight.
4 Mount into the frame, tack into place.

Plain-edge cushion

MATERIALS

■ Backing fabric 4in (10cm) larger than the finished design
■ Cushion pad 2in (5cm) larger than the finished design
■ Pins
■ Zip (optional)

1 After the canvas has been stretched, machine stitch two rows around the design ½in (12mm) from the edge of the worked area of canvas to prevent fraying. Trim to leave a 1in (2.5cm) seam allowance all around the design.
2 Cut the backing fabric to the same size as the trimmed canvas.
3 With the right sides of the fabric and canvas facing, tack or pin together, leav-

Plain-edge cushion

ing an opening on one side large enough to insert the cushion with a pad. Machine sides together carefully, as close as possible to the worked tapestry edge. Trim and oversew all raw edges, trim the corners. Turn the cushion right side out through the opening.
4 Insert the cushion pad and close opening with slip stitches along the seam line. If preferred, a zip can be stitched into the opening.

Decorative cord-edge cushion

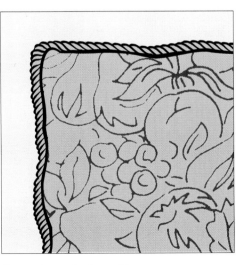

Decorative cord-edge cushion

MATERIALS

■ Backing fabric 4in (10cm) larger than the finished design
■ Cushion pad 2in (5cm) larger than the finished design
■ Decorative cord 2in (5cm) longer than the measurement round the outside edge of the finished design
■ Pins
■ Zip (optional)

1 Follow the instructions for a plain-edge cushion, but leave a 1in (2.5cm) opening along one side for the ends of the cord to be tucked in.
2 Bind the ends of the cord with sellotape to prevent fraying.
3 Slip stitch the cord around the edge of the cushion, neaten the ends by splicing or stitching then insert them into the opening and sew it up.

Piped-edge cushion

MATERIALS

■ Backing fabric 4in (10cm) larger than the finished design plus an extra piece large enough to cut bias strips 2in (5cm) wide, the length of the outer edge of the finished, stretched design
■ Piping cord no 3, 4in (10cm) longer than the measurement round the edge of the finished design
■ Cushion pad 2in (5cm) larger than the finished design
■ Pins
■ Zip (optional)

1 Cut 2in (5cm) wide bias strips of fabric and join together to make one strip the length required to cover the piping cord.
2 With wrong sides together, fold the bias strip in half, with the piping cord laid inside it. Tack strip together close to the cord to make piping edge.

Piped-edge cushion

3 Tack the piping edge onto the seam line on the right side of the cushion front. Join the ends by unravelling about ¾in (2cm) of the cord at both ends and cutting to different lengths before re-twisting to make a smooth join. Neatly hand stitch up the ends of the fabric covering.

4 Complete as for plain-edge cushion.

Needlecase

MATERIALS

❚ Backing fabric 4in (10cm) larger than the finished, stretched design
❚ Braid or piping 2in (5cm) longer than the measurement round the outside edge of the finished design (optional)
❚ Felt large enough to make four to six leaves to fit inside the needlecase
❚ Length of narrow ribbon for ties
❚ Pins
❚ Pinking shears

1 Machine stitch two or three rows around the design ½in (12mm) from the edge of the worked area of canvas to prevent fraying. Trim to leave a 1in (2.5cm) seam allowance.

2 Fold the seam allowance to the back of the canvas, mitre the corners and work herringbone stitches to attach it to the back of the canvas, taking care the stitches do not show on the right side.

3 If a decorative braid or piping is used, pin it to the turned edge of the needlecase and tack into place.

4 Cut the backing fabric ½in (12mm) larger than the finished work.

5 With the wrong sides of the fabric and canvas facing, pin together, folding in the turnings.

6 Cut narrow ribbon in half and tuck it into the centre edges, between backing fabric and canvas, then stitch in place.

7 Slip stitch the backing fabric to the needlecase.

8 If braid or piping is being used, slip stitch this to the outside edge, neatening the ends as appropriate.

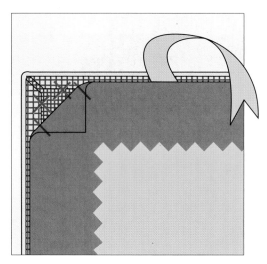

Needlecase, showing narrow ribbon placed between backing fabric and canvas

9 Use the pinking shears to cut the felt into four or six pieces, each ½in (12mm) smaller than the finished needlecase. Stab stitch to the centre of the needlecase to hold in place.

10 Fold needlecase in half, secure ties. If desired, stitch decorative braid or piping to centre of needlecase where it folds in half.

Curtain tiebacks

MATERIALS

❚ Buckram the same size as the finished stretched design or template
❚ Curtain interlining (or domette) the same size as finished design/template
❚ Lining fabric 4in (10cm) larger than the finished design
❚ Plain or decorative cord to fit the finished edges of the tiebacks plus 4in (10cm) extra
❚ Two rings per tieback
❚ Pins

1 Cut the buckram to the same size as the template or finished design area.

2 Iron the interlining onto the buckram, using a damp cloth. Trim the interlining to the edge of the buckram.

3 Machine stitch two rows round the design ½in (12mm) from the edge of the worked area of canvas to prevent fraying. Trim to leave a 1in (2.5cm) seam allowance all around the design.

4 Place the buckram on the wrong side of the canvas, with the interlining between the two, lining up with the finished edge of the design, and tack in place.

5 Clip into the canvas border, taking great care not to cut into the worked area. Dampen the edges of the buckram, then fold the clipped edges of the canvas over onto the damp edges of the buckram and iron down.

6 If decorative cord or any other trimmings are to be used, sew to edge of tiebacks with slip stitching.

7 Cut out a lining ½in (12mm) larger than the finished work. Pin to the tieback, fold under seam allowance then tack, neatening where necessary, slip stitch round edge.

8 Sew a ring onto the lining at the centre point of each of the tieback ends so that they are hidden from the right side.

Flat seat cover

▮ ⅛ or ¼in (2.5 or 5mm) thick foam the same size as the template or the finished stretched design

▮ Polyester wadding large enough to cover both sides of the foam

▮ Four lengths of tape or cord to tie cushion to the chair

▮ Backing fabric 4in (10cm) larger than the finished design

▮ Plain or decorative cord to fit round the finished edge of the design

▮ Pins

1 Cut out the foam to the same size as the template or worked design. Trim edges of foam so that they are neat and rounded.

2 Cut the polyester wadding into two pieces the same size as the foam. Place the foam between the two pieces of wadding to make a "sandwich", then catch stitch together to hold in place.

3 Machine stitch two or three rows around the design ½in (12mm) from the edge of the worked area to prevent fraying. Trim to leave a 1in (2.5cm) seam allowance around the design.

4 Cut the backing fabric to the same size as the trimmed canvas.

5 With the right sides of the fabric and canvas facing, tack or pin together, inserting the tapes or cord into the seams at the correct points so they will tie onto the chair, and leave an opening at the back large enough to insert the foam and polyester pad. Machine sides together carefully, as close as possible to the worked tapestry edge. Trim and oversew all raw edges, trim the corners. Turn the cushion right side out through the opening.

6 Insert the foam and polyester cushion pad and close opening with slip stitches.

Glasses case

▮ Lining fabric 2in (5cm) larger than the finished, stretched design

▮ Decorative cord 2in (5cm) longer than the measurement round the outside edge of the case (optional)

1 Machine stitch as close as possible around the design to prevent fraying.

2 Trim to leave a ⅞in (2cm) seam allowance all around the design.

3 Fold the seam allowance to the back of the canvas and carefully slip stitch to the back of worked stitches.

4 With the wrong sides of the canvas together, fold canvas in half. Herringbone or oversew together, leaving an opening at the top and making sure all unworked canvas threads are turned in.

5 Make a lining slightly smaller than the canvas case.

6 With right sides together, sew up bottom and side seams of lining.

7 Slip stitch lining to top opening of canvas to case. Tuck into case.

8 Finish by slip stitching the decorative cord round the outside edge.

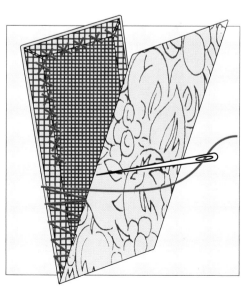

Stitching the sides of the glasses case

Footstool

▮ Round footstool (available from Stitchery)

▮ ⅜in (1cm) tacks

▮ Strong thread

1 Machine stitch two rows around the stretched design ¾in (2cm) from the edge of the worked area of canvas to prevent fraying. Trim to leave a 1½in (4cm) seam allowance.

2 Using a length of strong cotton threaded in a tapestry needle, sew a row of small running stitches round the circle of the design just inside the machine stitching, leaving enough thread at the beginning and end to act as draw-strings.

3 Place the canvas face down on a flat surface and centre the upholstered pad of the footstool onto the centre of the canvas.

4 Pull both ends of the draw-strings gently, easing the canvas round the edge of the pad as the thread is pulled tighter. Secure with a bow.

5 Ease out the gathers on the back of the footstool pad so there is an even finish round the edge.

6 Tack the canvas onto the underside of the pad ½in (12mm) from the edge, placing the tacks ½ to ¾in (12–20mm) apart.

$\mathscr{S}$TITCH $\mathscr{D}$IRECTORY

The most valuable rule to bear in mind when working stitches is the one which requires as much coverage on the back of the canvas as there is on the front. This ensures that a piece of work which may have taken months, even sometimes years, will be able to withstand more than a lifetime of daily wear and tear.

In the following stitch diagrams the needle is shown going into and coming out of the canvas in one movement, to show where the next stitch starts. However, I strongly recommend that all stitches are worked with a stabbing movement, with one hand feeding the needle down through the canvas and the other passing it back up.

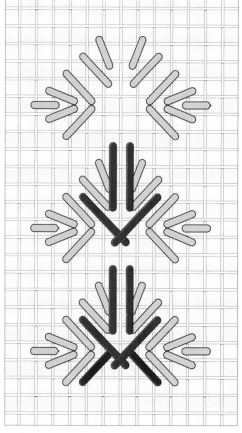

Following the diagram, work in three stages, as follows. Complete all stitches in the first colour, add the four large stitches in the second colour, then work the last two stitches in the third colour.

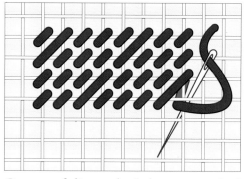

Groups of diagonal stitches are worked over 1,2,1 threads of canvas, filled in between with blocks of four tent stitches.

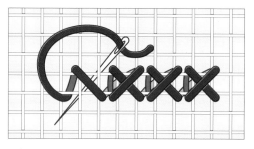

There are many methods of working this stitch and the simplest is to complete each cross before stitching the next. On single mono-thread canvas, work a diagonal stitch over two threads and complete the cross by working a second diagonal stitch in the opposite direction over the top of the first. All crosses must have the top stitch slanting in the same direction so that the stitches lie flat and have a smooth appearance.

On double-thread canvas, use the same method, working each stitch over the intersections of two close threads of canvas.

A group of seven diagonal satin stitches are worked in the same slanting direction to form a square over 1,2,3,4,3,2,1 threads of canvas. A variation can be obtained by alternating the direction of

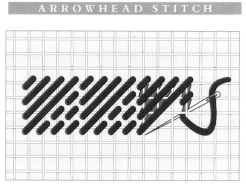

A group of four diagonal stitches worked over 1,2,3,4 intersections of canvas to form a triangle. Six tent stitches are worked to complete the pattern and form a square.

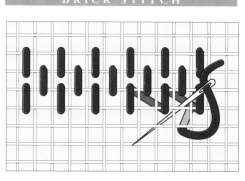

Rows of straight stitches are worked over two threads of canvas with a space of two threads of canvas between each stitch. The next row is started one thread below the first row. The rows interlock.

122

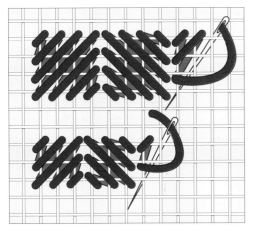

each group of stitches. For a smaller cushion, stitch five diagonal stitches over 1,2,3,2,1 threads of canvas.

FLORENTINE STITCH

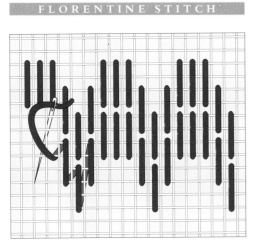

Rows of straight stitches are worked vertically over four threads of canvas, each stitch rising or falling by two threads. The return row interlocks into the first row, repeating the rise and fall of the original stitches.

FLOWER STITCH

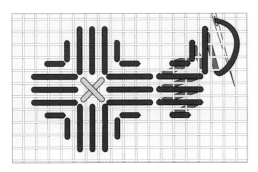

Straight satin stitches worked over 2,4,4,4,2 threads of canvas and worked round to form a flower. The centre is filled with a cross stitch.

GOBELIN STITCH (SLANTING)

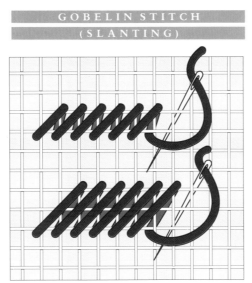

This diagonal stitch can be worked over a varying number of threads and inter-sections, usually no more than ten threads. Take care that the yarn remains untwisted, and stitches are worked with an even tension, so that they lie flat and even on the surface of the canvas.

GOBELIN STITCH (STRAIGHT)

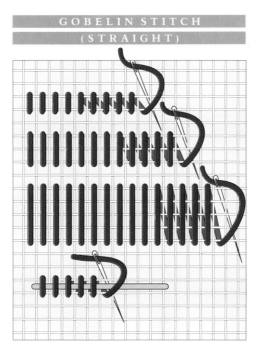

This straight stitch can be worked over any number of threads of canvas. To work a neat mitred corner, follow diagram below.

If a raised texture is needed, lay a strand of yarn along the canvas and work the straight gobelin stitches over the strand. It is important to work this stitch with an even tension and to keep the wool untwisted so that the stitches lie flat and even on the canvas.

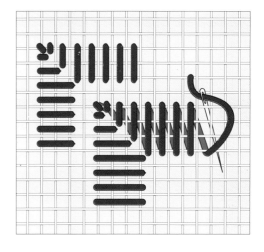

HUNGARIAN VARIATION STITCH I

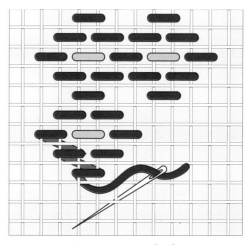

Eight stitches are worked over two threads of canvas to form a diamond. The centre of each pattern is filled with a straight stitch over two threads of canvas in a contrasting colour. Each diamond is linked to the next.

HUNGARIAN VARIATION II

Eight stitches are worked over one thread of canvas to form a diamond. The centre of each pattern is filled with straight stitches over 1,3,1 threads of canvas in a contrasting colour. Each diamond is linked to the next.

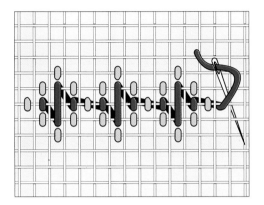

LEAF STITCH

Small Seven straight or diagonal stitches are worked over one or two threads or intersections of canvas. Start with a straight stitch over two threads of canvas and then work the other six stitches up to the tip of the leaf and back down to the base.

Large Seven straight or diagonal stitches are worked over three and two threads or intersections of canvas. Start with a straight stitch over three threads of canvas and work the other six stitches round to the tip of the leaf and back down to the base.

SCOTTISH VARIATION STITCH

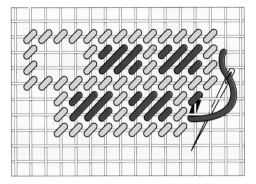

Work the outline of fourteen tent stitches first to form a framework and then fill in with slanting gobelin stitch over 1,2,2,1 intersections of canvas.

TENT STITCH

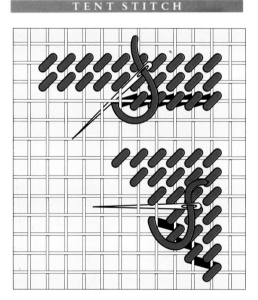

There are two ways of working this stitch: continental and basketweave (shown on mono and double canvas). All stitches must slant in the same direction.

Continental Work tent stitch in rows horizontally or vertically, using a slanting back stitch so that there is a long stitch on the back of the canvas. When working along a row to the left, stitches will be worked from below the thread to above the thread; and on the return row, working to the right, stitches will be worked from above the thread to below.

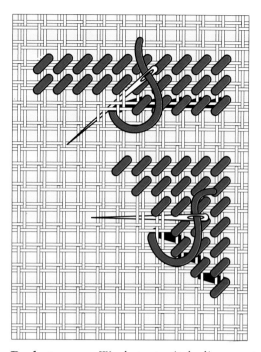

Basketweave Work tent stitch diagonally from the top corner. On 'down' rows, the needle is taken straight down under two horizontal threads of canvas. On 'up' rows, the needle is taken behind two vertical threads of canvas. Take care to work up and down rows alternately.

BEADING

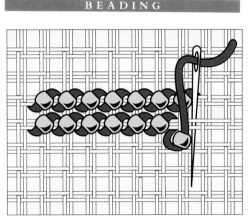

Using a double thickness of thread (not wool), apply each bead onto the canvas separately. Pick up the bead with the needle and work a diagonal stitch over two close threads of canvas. The beads will lie in the opposite direction to the tent stitch background, which is worked with three strands of crewel yarn.

THREAD CONVERSION CHART

APPLETON TO NEW ANCHOR

SHADE CONVERSION CHART

APPLETON	NEW ANCHOR	APPLETON	NEW ANCHOR	APPLETON	NEW ANCHOR
101	8588	465	8694	754	8366
102	8590	472	8132	755	8368
103	8592	474	8136	756	8400
104	8592	475	8102	757	8402
106	8596	478	9562	758	8424
145	8420	502	8216	759	8426
153	8896	504	8218	822	8690
155	8900	542	9172	825	8634
181	9632	543	9162	831	8968
182	9656	544	9164	832	8970
202	9594	545	9176	833	8972
205	8326	546	9204	835	9028
206	8262	551	8112	841	8036
221	9616	581	9644	842	9286
222	9618	585	9684	843	8018
223	8348	586	9664	844	8020
224	8400	588	9666	863	8310
226	8220	601	8542	872	8012
244	9218	603	8546	873	9252
253	9198	621	8252	874	9012
254	9168	622	8304	875	8702
256	9206	626	8162	877	8294
305	9644	647	8884	884	8584
311	9284	691	9322	941	8392
312	9286	694	8042	945	8436
313	9288	695	8060	963	9790
321	8706	696	8102	976	9662
322	8734	698	9450	991	8004
324	8738	711	8504	992	8006
326	8742	713	8508	996	8014
331	9322	716	8514		
351	9254	741	8714		
352	9058	742	8624		
353	9172	743	8626		
354	9174	744	8626		
355	9176	745	8628		
402	9016	746	8630		
461	8714	747	8632		
462	8686	751	8392		
463	8688	752	8362		
464	8632	753	8364		

STOCKISTS

*A*ll the canvas, wools and beads used in the patterns in this book are available from specialist needlework shops and the needlework departments of large stores. Stitchery kits are sold by over three hundred shops and stores in the UK including stores in the John Lewis Partnership. Some of the footstools shown in this book and a further selection of furniture for upholstering with finished canvases are also available from our stockists. The UK shops listed below are a selection of those who would be able to offer you expert advice and supply all your requirements as well as showing you the Stitchery range of tapestry kits. Many shops will supply you by mail order but please telephone them for details. For further information on stockists please contact Stitchery, 6 High Street, Thames Ditton, Surrey KT7 0RY (Tel 081 398 5550, Fax 081 398 8298). If you have any difficulty obtaining Appleton or Anchor threads or Mill Hill Beads, contact the manufacturers direct at the addresses below.

Appleton Bros Ltd (Yarns), Thames Works, Church Street, Chiswick, London W4 2PE (Tel 081 991 0711)

Coats Patons Crafts (Anchor), PO Box, McMullen Road, Darlington, Co Durham DL1 1YQ (Tel 0325 381010)

Maple Textiles (Beads), 188–190 Maple Road, Penge, London SE20 8HT (Tel 081 778 8049)

SCOTLAND
Christine Riley, 53 Barclay Street, Stonehaven, Kincardineshire AB3 2AR (Tel 0569 63238)

The Embroidery Shop, 51 William Street, Edinburgh EH3 7LW (Tel 031 225 8642)

The Glasgow Needlewoman, 111 Candleriggs, Glasgow G1 1NP (Tel 041 553 1933)

N. IRELAND
Busybodies, Audley Court, 120 High Street, Holywood, Co Down, N. Ireland BT18 9HW (Tel 0232 423756)

ENGLAND
Russells Needlework, 30 Castle Street, Carlisle, Cumbria CA3 8TP (Tel 0228 43330)

Spinning Jenny, Bradley, Keighley, W Yorks BD20 9DD (Tel 0535 632469)
(also at Market Place, Masham, nr Ripon, N. Yorks HG4 4EB, Tel 0765 689351)

Craft Basics, 9 Gillygate, York YO3 7EA (Tel 0904 652840)
(also at 2 Castle Gate, Helmsley, Yorks YO6 5AB: Tel 0439 71300)

Wye Needlecraft, 2 Royal Oak Place, Matlock Street, Bakewell, Derbys DE4 1EE (Tel 0629 815198)

Hepatica, 82a Water Lane, Wilmslow, Cheshire SK9 5BB (Tel 0625 526622)

Campden Needlecraft Centre, High Street, Chipping Campden, Glos GL55 6AG (Tel 0386 840583)

Hemsleys, 28 Steep Hill, Lincoln LN2 1LU (Tel 0522 514880)

The Stitch Shop, 15 The Podium, Northgate Street, Bath BA1 5AL (Tel 0225 481134)
(also at 5 Colonnades, Bath Street, Bath, Tel 0225 444880)

Mace & Nairn, 89 Crane Street, Salisbury, Wiltshire SP1 2PY (Tel 0722 336903)

Wessex Needlecraft, 8 Station Road, Parkstone, Poole, Dorset BH14 8UB (Tel 0202 735881)

The Tapestry Centre, 42 West Street, Alresford, Hants SO24 9AU (Tel 0962 734944)

Redburn Crafts & Needlework Centre, Squires Garden Centre, Halliford Road, Upper Halliford, Shepperton, Middlesex TW17 8RU (Tel 0932 788052)

LONDON
Liberty, Regent Street, London W1R 6AH (Tel 071 734 1234)

John Lewis, Oxford Street, London W1A 1EX (Tel 071 629 7711)

Harrods, Knightsbridge, London SW1X 7XL (071 730 1234)

Peter Jones, Sloane Square, London SW1W 8EL (Tel 071 730 3434)

Creativity, 45 New Oxford Street, London WC1A 1BH (Tel 071 240 2945)

Frances Cotton, 11 The Market, Greenwich, London SE10 9HZ (Tel 081 858 3309)

WHI Tapestry Shop, 85 Pimlico Road, London SW1W 8PH (Tel 071 730 5366)

AUSTRALIA
Altamira (Stitchery Kits), 34 Murphy Street, South Yarra, Victoria 3141 (Tel (03) 867 1240)

FRANCE
Voisine (Stitchery Kits), 12 rue de l'Eglise, 92200 Neuilly-sur-Seine (Tel (1) 46.37.54.60)

HONG KONG
Needle Works, A102 Villa Verde, 16 Guildford Road, The Peak, Hong Kong (Tel 849 6252)

ITALY
D & C Divisione Sybilla (Stitchery Kits), via Nannetti 1, 40049 Zola Predosa, Bologna (Tel (051 75.88.55)

NEW ZEALAND
The Stitching Company (Stitchery Kits), PO Box 74–269, Market Road, Auckland 5 (Tel (09) 524–9739)

SPAIN
Madial (Stitchery Kits), Principe de Vergara 82, 28006 Madrid (Tel 262 6073)

USA
Potpourri (Stitchery Kits and Appleton Yarns), PO Box 78, Redondo Beach, Ca 90277 (Tel 213 374 1267)

Susan Bates Inc (Anchor Wools), 212 Middlesex Avenue, Chester, Conn. 06412 (Tel 203 526 5381)

Gay Bowles Sales Inc (Mill Hill Beads), 1310 Plain Field Avenue, PO Box 1060, Janesville, WI 53547 (Tel 608 754 9466)

Access Discount Commodities, PO Box 156, Simpsonville, Maryland 21150

Chaparral, 3701 West Alabama, Suite 370, Houston, Texas 77027

Dan's Fifth Avenue, 1520 Fifth Avenue, Canyon, Texas 79015

The Elegant Needle Ltd, 7945 MacArthur Boulevard, Suite 203, Cabin John, Maryland 20818

Ewe Two Ltd, 24 North Merion Avenue, Bryn Mawr, PA 19010

Handcraft From Europe, PO Box 31524, San Francisco, Ca 94131-0524

The Jolly Needlewoman, 5810 Kennett Pike, Centreville, Delaware 19807

Louise's Needlework, 45 N. High Street, Dublin, Ohio 43017

Natalie, 144 N. Larchmont Boulevard, Los Angeles, Ca 90004

Needlepoint Inc, 251 Post Street, 2nd Floor, San Francisco, Ca 94108

Needle Works Ltd, 4041 Tulane Avenue, New Orleans, La 70119

Princess & The Pea, 1922 Parminter Street, Middleton, Wisconsin 53562

Sign Of The Arrow – 1867 Foundation Inc, 9740 Clayton Road, St Louis, Mo 63124

Village Needlecraft Inc, 7500 S Memorial Pkwy, Unit 116, Huntsville, Ala 35802

CANADA
Coats Bell, Canada (Anchor Wools), 1001 Roselawn Avenue, Toronto, Ont M6B 1B8 (Tel 416 782 4481)

Dick & Jane (Stitchery Kits and Appleton Yarns), 2352 West 41st Avenue, Vancouver, BC V6M2A4 (Tel 604 266 1090)

The Nimble Thimble (Stitchery Kits), 3201A Yonge Street, Toronto, Ontario M4N 2K9 (Tel 416 483 5462)

Fancyworks (Appleton Yarns), 104–3960 Quera Street, Victoria, BC V8X 4A3

Jet Handcraft Studio Ltd (Appleton Yarns), 1847 Marine Drive, West Vancouver, BC V7V 1J7

S.R. Kertzer Ltd (Appleton Yarns), 105a Winges Road, Woodbridge, Ont L4L 6C2

One Stitch At A Time (Appleton Yarns), Box 114, Picton, Ont K0K 2T0

The Silver Thimble Inc (Appleton Yarns), 64 Rebecca St, Oakville, Ont L6J 1J2

FURTHER READING

There are so many books on every conceivable aspect of needlework that one hardly knows where to begin, but the following is a selection of my own favourites, which I have found useful.

Beck, Thomasina *Embroidered Gardens* (Angus and Robinson, 1979)
The Embroiderer's Garden (David & Charles, 1988)
The Embroiderer's Flowers (David & Charles, 1992)

Benn, Elizabeth (Ed) *Treasures from the Embroiderers' Guild Collection* (David & Charles, 1992)

Clabburn, Pamela *Beadwork* (Shire Publications, 1980)

Fassett, Kaffe *Glorious Inspiration* (Century, 1991)

King, Donald *Samplers* Victoria & Albert Museum (HMSO, 1960)

Modes & Travaux *A Sampler of Alphabets* (Sterling, New York, 1987)

Proctor, Molly G. *Victorian Canvaswork* (Batsford, 1972)

Schoeser, Mary & Ruffey, Celia *English and American Textiles, From 1790 to the Present* (Thames & Hudson, 1989)

ACKNOWLEDGEMENTS

More than anyone else I have to thank my team of stitchers whose beautiful work and kind and gentle comments as they stitched my designs have made this book possible. They are Jane Brierley, Hilary Coe, Katie Dyson, Joan Fuller, Sybil Goodfellow, Rita Hughes, Pat Scottow, and Anne Watson.

For their never-ending support I thank Jane Formby and Jennifer Carr Jones who have lent me their work, my family and friends (especially Janet Haigh) who have encouraged me, given me inspiration and loaned me pieces from their needlework collections.

Thanks also to the Haines family, Angela, David and Nic, who are talented perfectionists and have so beautifully finished many of the needlework projects in this book. To Elind Frames Ltd, Beauchamp's Place, 91 Bridge Road, East Molesey, Surrey KT8 9HH (Tel 081 941 0300) who framed all of the samplers.

To Peter Armitage, known to us as 'Peter Wools', of Appleton Bros, and his staff, who have supported Stitchery for the last twelve years; their dedication and loyalty to their customers could never be equalled. My team at Stitchery, Pat Rattue and Jean and Frank Porter, who have managed to keep things in order even better without my constant interference. Thanks to Vivienne Wells of David & Charles for her quiet and persistent persuasion over the last three years. I hope I have been able to justify her faith in me.

My gratitude to all those who have worked on the design side of this book, supervised by Brenda Morrison at David & Charles – Peter Bridgewater, Tim and Zöe Hill, Angela Kirk, Ethan Danielson and Susan Rentoul.

Finally to Lis Barrett who made it all possible. She coaxed me to the very end, interpreted my manuscript but never changed the meaning and was always enthusiastic at the right moment.

Thank you.

INDEX

Page references in *italics* indicate illustrations